M000312082

# Always with Me

Copyright © 2018 Demeter Press

Individual copyright to their work is retained by the authors. All rights reserved. No part of this book may be reproduced or transmitted in any form by any means without permission in writing from the publisher.

Funded by the Government of Canada
Financé par la gouvernement du Canada

Demeter Press
140 Holland Street West
P. O. Box 13022
Bradford, ON L3Z 2Y5
Tel: (905) 775-9089
Email: info@demeterpress.org
Website: www.demeterpress.org


Demeter Press logo based on the sculpture "Demeter" by Maria-Luise Bodirsky, www.keramik-atelier.bodirsky.de

Printed and Bound in Canada

Front cover design: Peter Paré


Library and Archives Canada Cataloguing in Publication
Always with me : parents talk about the death of a child
/ Donna McCart Sharkey, editor.

Includes bibliographical references.
ISBN 978-1-77258-169-0 (softcover)

1. Children—Death—Psychological aspects. 2. Parents—
Psychology. 3. Bereavement—Psychological aspects. I. Sharkey,
Donna, editor

BF575.G7A38 2018          155.9'37085          C2018-903959-0

MIX
Paper from
responsible sources
FSC
www.fsc.org   FSC® C004071

# Always with Me

## Parents Talk about the Death of a Child

EDITED BY
Donna McCart Sharkey

DEMETER
DEMETER PRESS

# Table of Contents

# Acknowledgements

From the bottom of my heart, I thank the contributors to this anthology for sharing their poignant stories and for doing so with such openheartedness. I owe tremendous gratitude to my Bereaved Families group—Madeleine, Michel, Kim, Barb, Sylvie, Antoine, Elaine, Sean, Ingrid, Jane, and Dilys—who embraced the idea of this book from the beginning and never stopped asking how it was coming along. My heartfelt thanks to Maureen Cullingham, whose editing in the early stages was invaluable and to Chris Fox, who provided critical comments and suggestions. For their guidance and encouragement, my gratitude goes to Lynne van Luven and Kitty Lewis. Thank you to Carolyn Smart for the use of her lines in the epigraph. Much appreciation and a huge thank you to Andrea O'Reilly, my publisher at Demeter Press, who strongly supported this project, worked wonders, and did so at lightning speed. It was a privilege to work with Andrea, who has devoted so much of her life to issues surrounding motherhood. It is an honour to have my book included in her outstanding press. Enormous thanks to my sister, Arleen Pare, with whom I had many conversations about this project and who has been a wellspring of inspiration. Her encouragement, support, and clarity have sustained me throughout. Finally, my appreciation to my late parents, Tom and Irene McCart, and deep gratitude to my daughter, Renata, who is a woman of courage, and who knew and loved her older sister, Alessandra.

*To parents whose children have died before them*

*Nobody has ever measured, not even poets, how much the heart can hold.*

—Zelda Fitzgerald

*When one's own heart-child goes to death*
*What's left?*

—Carolyn Smart

# Introduction

DONNA MCCART SHARKEY

*When a child dies, you bury the child in your heart.*
—Korean proverb

WHEN I LOST MY DAUGHTER, I was still a mother, but different—a mother whose child has died. When people ask me now "how many children do you have?" I pause. What to say to this person?

A parent's worst nightmare—the death of a child.

I have lived every parent's worst nightmare, which is true of every parent in this anthology.

When my daughter, Alessandra, died three years ago, I was unmoored from reality. I clenched to life like someone stranded at sea. My breathing became shallow. My life emptied out. I needed to not forget my daughter's voice, her big smile, her effervescence, her deep loyalty, and how she mostly loved life, except when she didn't. Some friends surprised me with kindness and compassion. Others never acknowledged my child's death, the unsaid dangling in the air.

I started to make notes about my feelings, about my daughter and about life, on envelopes in my car, on scraps of paper beside my bed in the middle of the night—anytime, anywhere. Writing and reading were the places I went to. They were my way to try to come to terms with the impossible and untenable. I read every book I could find in the Ottawa Public Library and the University of Ottawa library on grief, on dying, on loss, and I still could not find any resonating personal account from a grieving mother's

1

point of view. Nothing spoke to me about my own sadness, and I could find few examples of parents telling their own stories of this type of pain. This inspired me to produce that book myself.

This book is what my reading became. Like me, parents contributing to this book wanted and needed to know other parents' experiences: how life goes on, how the pain is handled, and if it can be transformed. The book further opens these discussions, so often closeted. I hope this dialogue will extend beyond the closed doors of bereavement group meeting rooms and counsellor offices.

From the beginning, this project felt right. I was reassured by responses I received when I talked to people about the book. Some people looked horrified and said such things as: "How morbid, you shouldn't be talking about it" or "Couldn't you do something less dismal, less depressing?" or "Why would you ever do this?" I appreciated these comments. They set my resolve, and spurred me on just as much as the encouraging responses I got about the project. I thank all those who took the time to talk with me about this book.

This book confronts a life experience many people find hard to imagine. Everyone thinks of death at some point—at times, even their own death. Many people, at some point, imagine the death of their child, although almost no one wants to think it could ever happen. They say, "I can't imagine it." They say, "it's too painful to think about." We who have lost a child are the fear of every parent. We are the ones other parents never want to be. We are who we never wanted to be. Others may be afraid to say our child's name in front of us. And whereas other family members who have experienced loss have names like orphans or widows, we have no designation.

This anthology was borne of love and grief, each story written through tears and into deep memories. It was also borne of change—family structure that has fractured, holidays that will never be the same, a Mother's Day or a birthday six years later that can sideswipe. Tears come, even much later, unexpectedly. The emotional shock can return and can still numb.

Some parents told me they wanted to write their story, but then they found it too heartbreaking. One mother said to me, "after much thought, I just can't do it. I sit down and try to write, but

I just cry." I understood. Writing my own story left me depleted each time I wrote. At times, I sobbed looking at the words as they formed on my computer screen.

For all of us who contributed to the book, writing these stories was a return to raw emotion. We were on our own, writing. During the writing process, parents told me what it was like for them. One woman said, "Writing my story makes me realize I'm one of the walking wounded." Another said, "As I'm writing this, I'm moving through some dark times. We all know these times so well." And another mother said, "I'm struggling to express in words my ineffable experience of grief. I've been procrastinating. It's not easy, but I need to tell the story."

The writers in this anthology tell how the death of a child is different from other losses. They describe the shock and devastation, their emergence from mourning, the maelstrom of their inner landscapes, and how grief and loss are worked through. They detail their coping strategies. They talk about their isolation. Guilt, despair, fear, depression, regrets, and relationship changes are dissected. Life after six months, one year, ten years. Sorrow that brings them to their knees.

They chronicle how it takes time to be comfortable again in large groups, to breathe more loosely, to taste food, to sit up straight, to make a joke, and to be with people without thinking that what's going through their mind is "I'm talking to a mother whose child has died." Authors talk about how they attempt to make sense of their lives, their new perspectives on the world, and their place in it—their indelibly altered lives.

For each parent, the story is a labour of love and a labour of grief. Barb Duncan starts her chapter "Guess It's Time to Put It Down" by talking about the difficulty of writing about this topic. Suzanne Corbeil talks about the pull of how much of a child's life story ought to be told in order to understand the parent's grief: "How can I begin to talk about the grieving process without telling the story of the life that was lost?"

Others talk about the shock of being told their child is dead. A police officer knocked on Tara McGuire's door and asked her if William Holden Courage is her son: "That was all I needed to hear. In that instant, looking in his damp reluctant eyes, I knew it was the worst possible news. When those words hit my heart…the world, the universe as I knew it, shattered." Randie Clark received a phone call from her son's friend. "David was robbed tonight, and there was a knife, and he was stabbed, and he's dead."

Cathy Sosnowsky asks if she and her husband could have saved their child from death at the same time as knowing they could not have. Her son died in the late evening: "If we'd stayed awake, could we have saved him? Of course not."

The last time Stephanie Gilman spoke with her daughter was during a phone conversation. She told her that they would continue talking when she got home: "We would never talk again. Before I got home that afternoon, Jesse hanged herself in her bedroom."

Jacquelyn Johnston asks the reader a hard question. "What if your two children died ten days apart in separate accidents? How would you feel?"

Some parents discuss the difficulty of going on after their child's death. Becky Livingston gives her reason: "But there's Charlotte. My living daughter."

Parents discuss what life is like shortly after the funeral and then afterward. Lorna Thomas tells us that she was barely able to leave the house: "I lost interest in everything…. I cried constantly, retreating to the spare room in our house. One day I could not stop crying, a whole day of tears." And Judith Maguet faced her first Christmas without her son with trepidation.

Three years after her son died, Martha Royea sometimes thinks, "I don't believe he's gone. I think, Rick hasn't called for a while. I think, one of these days the phone will ring." Nine years after her son Jesse died, Ingrid Draayer describes life as "living in a parallel universe among the whole nuclear families." For Micheline Lepage, "the pain and emptiness never go away—they just get more manageable."

Most stories we read on other topics end with a resolution. The lonely adolescent comes out of her shell. The couple, unhappy for years, do get a divorce and happily start anew. The shy woman lands a dream job. We all cheer. But after the death of a child, there is rarely this kind of turnaround. The usual story arc is more like a beleaguered and ill-equipped march through an unknown land, a long slough. The story rarely wraps up tidily. Nevertheless, as Leonard Cohen wrote, "There is a crack in everything. That's how the light gets in."

I am grateful to all the contributors for their openness in sharing intimate and difficult aspects of their lives. Each of these stories is an act of courage, each an act of generosity. I trust that this book will support those who have experienced a child's death in their own lives. Whether you are reading this because you have a child who has died, or you're a family member, a friend, colleague, or someone with a professional or a general interest in the topic, I hope that reading this anthology will inform and open up the topic more naturally and candidly.

# 1.
## Objects We Hold

MARTHA ROYEA

We set such store by objects. They're what we have left of the dead: vestiges of the person we knew. We touch these things and our bodies remember their faces, their voices, their flesh. We dance with a box of ashes in our arms, and the one we loved breathes into our neck, or suckles at our breast, or tells us a story we didn't know before, of need and longing, or of happiness or hope, or of going away now, or not quite yet. We wear their rings, the bracelets they gave us, and their old shirts or hats or jackets—clothing where the smell of them lingers. We hold them and we dance, and over time they become lighter, lighter as our arms and our hearts make room.

# 2.
# Jesse's Story

STEPHANIE GILMAN

MY DAUGHTER'S STORY STARTS at her birth—two months
early, 1480 grams (three pounds two ounces), and with some
health challenges. Although she came home after only a month in
hospital, it soon became apparent that her development lagged. She
was late to crawl, walk, and talk. Communication was especially
difficult, leading to group and private speech therapy, and special
education classes. Despite these challenges, Jesse loved learning. She
would observe and listen intently. Reading came easily to her, and
she devoured books, reading her favourite ones many times. She
would get excited about an idea or concept, dragging the closest
adult to examine and share in her discovery. The connection would
often need to be interpreted, and she would beam with pleasure
when her intention was understood. She particularly enjoyed history and the natural world, and desired to be an archaeologist—a
career of which she could dream, if not pronounce.

Then at age twelve, she was diagnosed with leukemia. Though
no picnic, the disease was diagnosed in its early stages, and the
treatment regimen was a limited round of chemotherapy followed
by a cord blood stem cell transplant. She met this demanding
challenge with determination, finding enjoyment in the most difficult circumstances. Being confined to a hospital bed meant few
limits on television and the Discovery Channel. Recovery included
some setbacks, including infections and a feeding tube, and was
exhausting for her. Jesse was often fatigued, reading and napping
on the couch after school. She persevered, as she knew that when
she was well enough she would be given a dog—she eventually

chose a dachshund who loved to cuddle with her on the couch. She also enjoyed a Children's Wish trip to Greece. She saw for herself the source of history and myth at the Acropolis, Crete, Mount Olympus, and Delphi.

Her interest in history and in myth developed into a love of fantasy. She loved comics and movies, such as *The Avengers* and *Lord of the Rings*, which led to her participating in medieval sword fighting and festivals. She was a member and volunteer with Girl Guides and for a camp for kids with cancer. She played the piano and sang in the school choir. She expressed herself creatively through art and crafts.

In many ways Jesse was a typical teenager. She shirked her chores and her schoolwork, and preferred to either read or watch videos online. But her needs and desires were often difficult to understand. She continued to be stubborn, and although she did not communicate well with verbal or written language, she seemed to expect everyone to understand her. When she couldn't find the words to express herself she would scowl, stamp her foot, and give a harrumph of displeasure. She relied on her actions and body to communicate her feelings. What any teenager is thinking is a mystery to most parents, and Jesse often remained an enigma.

With support, Jesse was working toward her high school diploma. One exam week, she insisted that she had completed all of her work and was looking forward to a few days of break prior to her one exam. I wondered aloud if her teachers would agree and if she should return to school to ensure that everything was complete. Jesse assured me that if she needed to complete anything, she still had two days to return to school. I agreed a day's break was fair. We had just celebrated her five-years-cancer-free milestone, and we were tired from that excitement and the end of term.

I checked with the teachers. Jesse had one outstanding assignment. She had completed the art project, but the written explanation was missing. Since written expression was Jesse's particular difficulty, it did not surprise me that this portion of the assignment was incomplete. What concerned me was the teacher's report of Jesse's poor attitude and behaviour in the class regarding the assignment.

On my lunch break, I called Jesse to discuss the missing assignment and expressed my disappointment over her behaviour in class. I suggested that she forgo the Internet that afternoon and consider her assignment. Jesse reacted very strongly, growling into the phone. She could not communicate clearly. I changed my tactic and said that she seemed very upset, and I made some suggestions for calming activities, such as a walk or playing music. I said not to worry about it, and we would talk when I got home. Jesse did not say much in response but sullenly agreed.

We never talked again. Before I got home that afternoon, Jesse hanged herself in her bedroom. She was seventeen.

Jesse did not leave any explanation. Many believe she did not understand the permanence of her act. I would like to believe this is true. In the fantasy world, heroes live to see another day. There was some writing in her room in the fan fiction genre expressing how she had failed her fellow superheroes, but I do not know when she wrote it or if it was intended as a message.

Being a mother means guiding, encouraging, and disciplining when necessary, but above all, it means protecting. I did not protect my daughter from her difficulties. I encouraged her to put forth her best effort every day. Perhaps she felt that she had given her best effort and that she had failed. Or perhaps she felt a loss of identity after recovery from cancer. Or perhaps she was angry—at me, school, or others in her life. I will never know.

I continually review our last few days and conversations. Was there something I missed? What if I had said things differently? Would it have made a difference? I will never know. It is the not knowing that seems so hard and that fuels the guilt.

I was her mother, but we were buddies. I thought I knew her better than anyone. I had come to realize that it would be very difficult for Jesse to participate in a traditional workplace environment or to live independently any time soon. I hoped that she would be able to go to college, but that would have taken considerable time and effort. We would face our difficulties and problem solve together. We would work and play and travel and love and laugh and have fun. We would be buddies for a long time yet.

I miss my girl so much. All I want is to have her back with me to talk, to laugh, to snuggle on the couch, to watch movies. I want to drive her to activities. I want to get frustrated and insist she walk the dog, clean the bathroom, and do her homework. I want to hear her say "mo-ther" in the tone of voice that says you don't know anything. I want to feel her arms around me, see her sweet smile, and hear her say I love you.

I would do anything.

# 3.
# Different Worlds

SUZANNE CORBEIL

*There's so many different worlds*
*So many different suns*
*And we have just one world*
*But we live in different ones.*
　　　　　　　—"Brothers in Arms," Dire Straits

HOW CAN I BEGIN to talk about the grieving process without telling the story of the life that was lost?

As far back as I can remember, my dream was to have a caring husband and a house full of children. For the most part that dream has come true. I have a loving husband, four children, two stepchildren, and a granddaughter; I have the life I've always dreamed of.

By the age of twenty-five, I was married, and after a few months of trying to conceive, I came down with a terrible flu. I saw my doctor, who told me my flu would someday walk and talk. And so went my first two pregnancies. Luckily, the sickness eventually passed and the rest of the nine months went exceptionally well for my two eldest children, my daughters. With my third child, everything was different. At first I thought it was impossible I was pregnant again. After all, I didn't have a flu. My doctor explained the difference to me by saying before it was likely that my body was reacting to the hormones of my developing child—I became sick with a girl, not with a boy.

I knew from the beginning that my fourth child was different. I was sure beyond a doubt that this fourth child would be another son. For the next thirty weeks, I fondly called my growing belly *Adam*.

On 22 April 1993, after a very fast and relatively easy labour, the attending physician looked at me and said, "Congratulations you have a beautiful baby girl!"

"Are you sure?" I said.

He laughed and said, "In my limited experience, I am sure she is a girl."

After calling this little person Adam for so long, I struggled to name this girl. But in a moment of knowing, it was decided, she would be Rebecca Danielle-Adam to honour her story.

This child of mine had been a boy and was now a girl, but that's just the beginning.

At the age of five, Rebecca was diagnosed with a form of atypical epilepsy. This disability shaped much of her childhood. The seizures and the medication to treat it affected her in subtle yet significant ways. At times, it affected her memory or challenged her ability to learn. Although she succeeded in passing all her grades, it was never easy. She was a fun loving, energetic tomboy of a girl who always had friends, but she often felt she was on the sidelines. Never part of the in-crowd, she often experienced hurtful isolation and bullying, but she always pushed on.

Her father and I separated when she was six. I did my best to shelter her from the difficulty of that fracture in our family, but she never found it easy to navigate. Despite being deeply loved by each of us, she felt as torn as the relationship between her father and me.

At the age of ten, her specialists believed her to be free of epilepsy, and she was weaned off the antiseizure medications. But the effects of hundreds of seizures and prolonged use of medications meant that she still struggled with cognitive tasks. Even with her challenges, Rebecca enrolled in college, played goalie for a hockey team, held part-time jobs, and got her driver's license. She was determined to fulfill her dream of being independent and self-sufficient.

Then, at the age of eighteen, Rebecca's epilepsy took a turn for the worse, and her life became even more difficult. Over the next four years, she underwent two neurosurgeries and multiple medication changes in an attempt to minimize the impact of epilepsy on her life. All the while she continued to struggle with something even more profound and difficult: her journey of self-discovery. She began to feel conflicted about who she was, and her first step was identifying herself as a lesbian. That was only the beginning of her journey that eventually led her to acknowledge her true self was, in fact, male. Thus began a three-year journey to become who she had always been meant to be—Adam.

She had come full circle: conceived as a boy (in my mind), born as a girl, and now living as a transgender man.

After declaring his gender, Adam really blossomed. In becoming his own person, everyone noticed how much happier he seemed. In fact, 2016 began full of hope and optimism. He completed his second neurosurgery in November 2015, and felt better than he had in years. He was making plans for new beginnings, including going back to school. Adam lived for two seizure-free months following surgery, until the day he died.

On 22 January 2016, Adam, left alone for a few minutes in a hot tub, had a seizure and drowned.

That night and the following two days are a fog in my memory. We received the call that he had suffered another seizure and was being transported to the hospital. Then we arrived at the emergency unit only to be told that it was not simply a seizure but that he had drowned and his heart had stopped. We were told it took several minutes to get his heart to start again and he may not make it through the night. My family went from happy optimism to devastation in a mere flurry of moments. I was numb.

Adam spent two days in ICU on life support until finally declared brain dead on 24 January 2016.

The blur of the days that followed his death was just an evolution of the numbness I had been feeling, or perhaps not feeling. My days were filled with so many things to do. On automatic pilot, always being a take-action person, I just did things:

*Share the news.*
*Organ donation.*
*Funeral arrangement.*
*Greet family and friends.*
*Care for Adam's friends.*

*Plan a celebration of his life.*
*Build his casket and fill it with his most treasured things.*
*Arrange care for his dog, Dallas, and cat, Kitty.*
*Take care of paperwork, phone, Internet, bank, landlord.*
*Empty his apartment and dispose of his things.*
*Eat ... sleep ... cry ...*

Then came the void, the quiet, the emptiness, the regret, the guilt, and the most profound sadness I can describe. All the while, I felt I was the mom, the wife, the daughter, the grandmother, the sister who needed to be strong for others. That's what I thought I had to be: strong.

I am and always will be Adam's mom. During his twenty-two years of life, I had spent so much of my time and energy with him that now the emptiness of his absence is crippling. Adam and I spoke often and communicated daily through text messages and email. Suddenly the messages had stopped. I have since come to understand the saying "silence is deafening."

In the depths of silence, I worked to fill the void. The voices in my head and in my heart got louder. *How could this have happened? How did I get to this moment in my life? Did I see this coming? Why did I not follow through with having Adam over for dinner that Thursday night? Did I hug him last time I saw him? What did his voice sound like? What was he thinking the moments before he died? Did he know I loved him? Was I a good mother? Could I have done anything different or better? Did my advice somehow lead him to his death?*

I slowly realized that Adam's story had changed on that fateful day, but it did not end. His life ended with his last breath, but his life continues to have meaning, and his actions and decisions radiate beyond that moment. The extent of his impact on the world was something that would take me several months to understand.

The unconditional love and support from friends and family surrounded me. I can't even begin to imagine how hard it would have been if I hadn't had these people in my life. Some offered their prayers; others brought food and gifts, and others sent cards and flowers. They planted trees, and they travelled from far and wide to be with my family. They offered advice and support, anything they could do. I really have no way of knowing how much that affected my experience, but I do know that I was overwhelmed and appreciative beyond belief.

I have learned that grief is personal and unique for each person. I felt that this pain was mine and mine alone. No one could truly know how I felt, what I needed, or what I should do; I had to figure this out on my own. Even my husband, whose love was my rock and source of solace, did not truly understand.

So many people don't know what to say or do. I did, however, feel that there were a few gestures particularly meaningful to me. Every week for months, one friend sent a text message saying she was thinking of me. She set up a credit at a local caterer so I could get a meal when I did not feel like cooking. On Adam's birthday, and then again out of the blue, months later, she sent me a bouquet of flowers. When I finally found the energy to send her a message of thanks and apologized for not responding sooner, her response was "I didn't expect you to; I just wanted you to know I was here for you."

Another friend suggested I consult with a grief counsellor or a support group. I decided to try the counsellor she recommended. I met with him for several months, and it was helpful in a few ways. He provided me with a safe space to say anything without judgment. I brought my husband to one session, and we learned that his desire to protect me from my pain made it hard for me to grieve with him. Recognizing that difficulty allowed us to have a better understanding of how grief was putting a wedge in our relationship. I have learned that many marriages fall apart after the loss of a child. I need to be sure that mine does not; it is too important to me.

The words of Adam's transition counsellor keep ringing in my ears: "You will need to grieve the loss of Rebecca before you can fully accept Adam." In a moment of reflection, I realized I had not grieved the loss of my daughter, and now I had lost my son. I was suddenly aware that I was impossibly grieving the loss of two children; the burden of grief was weighing me down.

Something else I know now is that as much as every individual is different, so too will be their experience with grief. There is no roadmap; there is no book or wise counsel that can show you the way through your grief. Each of us has to dig deep within to find a reason to get up in the morning, to keep moving forward, and to have the desire to live on. Another thing I know is that life will never be the same again.

After losing Adam, my other children have become even more important to me, if that were possible. I worried for their wellbeing and sought out their companionship. For many years, it was me and my kids, and now more than ever, I needed them close to me.

Adam's short life left a very small estate that provided a modest inheritance for his siblings, and with that gift, the four of us decided to book a vacation together. It was an amazing time to connect through our stories, our grief, and our journeys forward. We laughed, we cried, we remembered stories. We drank to Adam and honoured his memory every day. It was during that time that I wrote the story of Rebecca and Adam to share with family and friends, many of whom had only known my child as either Rebecca or Adam. It was a hard piece for me to write, but it was also therapeutic. I felt good about telling his story of triumph over obstacles and his amazing strength of character. It reminded me that he was not perfect; he was just a typical child trying to find his way.

I know I have to work through the pain, or so the theory goes. I could not just stay home and be alone with my grief, so I decided to return to work just three weeks after Adam died. I needed the distraction. I was fortunate to have an understanding and supportive employer and amazing staff. They allowed me to be at work and contribute only to the extent I was able. I found that I was exhausted at the end of each day and beyond exhaustion at the end of the week, so I reduced my workload to four days a week. I have kept that schedule and don't expect I will ever return to work fulltime again.

It's funny how perspective changes, priorities get reordered, and things that once seemed important seem totally insignificant now. It was important for me to continue to be distracted. I needed to keep busy so that I could pace my way through my grieving journey. I began a labour of love by transforming my backyard into a garden of memories. I spent hours, days, and weeks digging, planting, and sowing. As Adam's garden took shape, it offered me a Zen-like space to sit with my grief. It attracted birds, butterflies, and bees.

I invited family and friends to contribute to the garden. Plants, statues, stepping stones, and shells were added. In the spring, a family of cardinals, which I had rarely seen in the past, moved in. They have come to symbolize Adam. The garden is now a place where I can go to feel safe in my grief and to remember the emptiness of my loss, and find some peace and joyful quiet.

In my grief, I am searching for Adam in the world. I want to believe that his spirit will visit me from "the other side." I am desperate to feel Adam's presence, but I cannot. I am envious that Adam's father boasts of receiving messages or feeling Adam's presence. How can it be that I was so connected to him in life, yet I cannot feel him in death? It is painful for me to say that I feel nothing. All I know is that he is gone. Is it my grief that prevents me from feeling, or my head, or maybe it just won't be? Is he in heaven? Is he with the angels? Does his spirit live on? I want to believe, but I find I am unable. I do not know what to believe or to hope for.

Several months after Adam died, I ventured to see a woman who claims to connect with angels. She told me Adam was with me and wanted me to know that he was ok. Despite wanting to believe her words, my grief kept me from accepting her messages.

One day, I received an anonymous letter through the Trillium Foundation, which manages organ donation in Ontario, from the recipient of Adam's heart. I find it impossible to explain the complex mix of feelings I experienced. Since receiving the letter, I have come to be grateful that Adam gave the gift of life to another human being. I am happy to know that the recipient is someone who Adam would have genuinely liked, with so many interests and attributes that remind me of him.

In the short time that Adam was able to drive, he enthusiastically signed his organ donation card. He told me that if something ever happened to him, why shouldn't someone else benefit? I am proud that his decision to donate his organs, his final act of love, has profoundly changed the life of another. However, knowing his heart recipient has been bittersweet. It is incredibly hard for me to see how happy and thankful he and his family are while we are still reeling from our loss. Adam's dad has decided to embrace this stranger, and he became part of his life. For me, it is different.

I do not wish him anything but the best, but it is too painful for me to be in his life.

Adam has also given the gift of life to two women who received his liver and his kidneys. I struggle with wanting to reach out to them to tell them how happy Adam would be to know that their lives are better because of him, but something keeps me from doing it.

People say to me, "things must be getting easier." I can't agree. What I would say is that my grief is evolving.

Every morning, as I put the necklace holding his ashes around my neck, I bid him good day and allow myself a moment of grief. I think of him often throughout my day—still accompanied by the pain of loss, but sometimes with remembered happy moments we shared. Thoughts and memories of this child I miss desperately are becoming a normal part of my daily life.

There are times when I hear a siren or a bird, when I sit in a hot tub or drive by a familiar spot, that I begin to sob uncontrollably. The pain remains tethered to my soul. It is said that we hold onto the pain because we are afraid to let it go. I think that is true for me. I need to learn how to live without Adam's presence, to live with just his memory. I pray that over time the memories will come back in full colour and sound.

Adam's story continues to have a ripple effect. His gift of life was written about in a number of newspapers to underscore the importance of organ donations. His story was written in *Voices for Epilepsy* to highlight the dangers of daily living to those who suffer from the disease. And he continues to inspire others in the transgender community to find the courage to be who they truly are.

I have come to believe that from the first moment when the spark of Adam's life was lit until the day he died, his journey was meant to be. I have a distinct memory of the night that my relationship with Adam's father began. I was listening to "Brothers in Arms" by Dire Straits. The words and melody touched me so deeply that night that I became very emotional, especially the line "every man has to die." Those lyrics have come back to haunt me in such a way that I believe I knew something profound was about to happen in my life.

This son-come-daughter-come-son of mine had a brief but meaningful life, and it continues to make a difference. For that,

I am thankful. But the loss of my youngest child continues to be the greatest burden I will ever carry. My life will move on, and I will continue to make the most of it with only the memories of the years I had with this special child of mine.

If I could, I would change the course of events in a moment—but I can't. Adam's life was meant to lead to his organ recipients so that their lives could continue. Adam's life and death have purpose—maybe he had an even greater purpose than most—and in that, I find some comfort. I know that Adam would be so proud of himself that he made such a difference in the world.

# 4.
# I Can't Imagine It

LORNA THOMAS

"FAMILY, FRIENDS SEARCH for Missing Man," reads the headline I look at the photograph. It is a picture of my only son, Alex. I am sitting on the edge of my bed reading the newspaper holding my breath. I set the paper down carefully in a box on the floor, beside the other clippings. I lie on the cool sheets of my bed and close my eyes. It is quiet in the room. I am holding my breath. I sit up again and reach for another newspaper, another headline. "Search for Missing Edmonton Man Called Off." I lie back on the bed. I cry until I am exhausted, so congested that I can barely breathe. I pull the pillow over my face so the neighbours won't hear me screaming.

A year later, I am sitting on that same bed with my laptop perched on the same pillow. Beside me is the same box. It is now full to the top with objects: several personal journals, handouts about bereavement, family photo albums and home movies, my hope scrapbook, books on death and dying, cards and messages from friends, and more newspaper clippings—some about Alex and some about the advocacy work I now do. I begin excavating the box. It is like an archaeological dig: uncovering precious memories of Alex's twenty-four years of life; finding clues or new evidence that will help me make sense of his death; re-reading my lists of reasons to keep on living. How does a mother go on after the death of her child? How can I make peace with the fact that my boy, my Alex, died by suicide?

This is the story of how I lived through that first year. And because grief is always about two people, this is also the story of a wonderful young man who loved life, but who, in the end, was unable to fulfil the kind of life he yearned for.

## ALEX THOMAS-HAUG (23 JULY 1987 – 14 MAY 2012)

*Who is the best, the very, very best, the very best little boy in the world? It's Alexander, Alexander, Alexander Thomas-Haug!*

This is the ditty I would sing to Alex when he was little. He was a calm baby and a happy toddler—my red-haired, blue-eyed pumpkin, who seldom cried except when he slipped and bumped his head on our hardwood floors.

Alex had doting grandparents who gave him horsey rides and created shadow puppets on his bedroom wall. His cousin Carrie started taking him skiing when he was only five. When he was a first grader, his father Phil Haug took him to the lake for canoe rides and adventures in the woods. His sister Cayley, who was two and a half years younger, would act out plays and dance with him.

Alex's red hair often made him the target of unwanted attention and sometimes bullies. As he got older, he would often wear a toque or ball cap, perhaps to hide his hair. In high school, Alex was an honours student who loved books, dressed stylishly, and was very popular with the girls When he was in grade eleven, he was scouted to be a fashion model; he was that handsome. But he didn't want to be a model; he wanted to be a snowboarder.

After high school, Alex moved from our home in Edmonton, Alberta, to the mountains of Banff and Lake Louise, along with several of his close guy friends. He worked in the service industry and became an excellent snowboarder. In retrospect, I wonder if Alex didn't have aspirations to be a professional boarder. But running low on money, and bowing to parental pressure, he returned to Edmonton after two years. With the promise of big money in the oil and gas industry, he chose to work in the trades.

We noticed that Alex's personality began to change as he was training and working as a welder. Hard work and long hours in a noisy, hot environment took its toll. His use of alcohol and marijuana increased. He appeared depressed, and was often irritable and negative. When I expressed my worry, Alex explained it away with a ready excuse: a breakup with a girlfriend or exhaustion from a sixty-hour workweek. After reading a brochure in my doctor's office, I brought up the possibility of mental illness, specifically depression and a bipolar condition. Alex read the article, nodded, but quickly changed the subject. Like many young adults, Alex didn't want to think about mental health. He believed his struggles were part of growing up, and perhaps he thought speaking about his problems and asking for help would be a sign of weakness.

Just before Christmas 2011, Alex had a snowboard accident and badly injured his knee. He was no longer able to get to the slopes, which robbed him of the activity he enjoyed most in life. Working nights in mid-winter, he became more and more withdrawn from us.

## MOTHER'S DAY: 12 MAY 2012

The last time I saw Alex was on Mother's Day. He had planned a special family activity that we had never tried before: go-karting. We picked him up at his place, and I was so relieved to see him. I had been anxious and worried since the time I'd seen him a few days before. He had been working such long hours, and he told us that he wasn't eating or sleeping properly.

As Cayley and Phil went zooming around the track in their go-karts, Alex and I chatted a bit as we waited our turn. He told me his roommates were moving out of the house they shared. I asked about his future plans. He said nothing. He just looked off into the sky; his pale blue eyes were fixed and flat, lacking the sparkle that had been there throughout his life. I often find myself thinking about that look. Was he imagining himself in a new place?

Alex came back to our house for supper. He presented me with bath products and a homemade Mother's Day card. His friends were playing a concert that evening, so after dinner he rushed out the door to pick up a friend. Early the next morning, he went missing.

We found out later that he partied all night, decided not to drive, and was dropped off at his house at 4:00 a.m., but he had forgotten his keys. He phoned the people still at the party and asked them to bring his keys, but they failed to do so. That morning when Alex's roommates found out that he wasn't at the party house and wasn't at home, they were worried but thought he might have gone to another friend's place. The next day Alex's employer phoned to let me know Alex hadn't shown up for work and hadn't returned his calls. I soon discovered that Alex had been missing for twenty-four hours. We called the police and then quickly organized a search.

Over a period of four days, hundreds of friends, neighbours, strangers, as well as police officers and search and rescue volunteers, set out to find Alex; thousands more spread the word on social media. During this time, one of Alex's friends told me that Alex had been using cocaine and speed. I was shocked. I soon found out that many people, friends and family, knew that Alex had been using hard drugs. They said they'd been worried about him. A few shared their concerns with him but many did not. Perhaps stigma and ignorance about drugs prevented those people from talking to him about it, or maybe they were afraid of losing his friendship. Possibly they underestimated the extent of his situation, or if they did know how serious it was, maybe they were unsure of how to help. Alex likely did not talk about his drug use because of shame or fear of losing his job. Whatever the reasons, Alex stayed silent. Many people in the know didn't talk to Alex, and they didn't talk to me. They had decided, "Don't tell Lorna." When I did find out, I lashed out with my fists, smashing the dashboard of my car, then the pillows in my room, and then I started slapping my own face. Hard.

The next morning, six days after Alex disappeared, two police officers came to the door. Alex's body had been found in a ravine close to the house. He had died by suicide, using a cat leash rope from his backyard to hang himself. There was no note. We will never know if his suicide was impulsive or planned.

When the police delivered the news, I was silent. I did not cry as I received hugs from family members who immediately came to the house. I prepared a statement for the media who were gathering close by. Stoically, I thanked everyone who had helped with the search. But when the television interviewer asked me how I was feeling, I stared at him, turned, and walked away.

## LATE SPRING 2012

*When you died, I died too, and with the death of us both, it took me a long time to come back to life, and I have to work at it still.*

After Alex's funeral, I could barely leave the house. I lost interest in everything. I couldn't read a book or write in my journal. I couldn't work. I lost fifteen pounds. I cut my hair short. I found it difficult to be in crowds. I got sick, and after several doctor's appointments and tests, I was diagnosed with rheumatoid arthritis. I cried constantly, retreating to the spare room in our house. One day I could not stop crying, a whole day of tears.

People were so concerned about my wellbeing. They dropped off nourishing food, interesting books, and flowers. They offered massages and cards with kind words. Others, including my daughter Cayley and my cat Lulu, would simply sit with me as I cried. Some friends stayed away—saying they were busy or they were giving me space. A month after Alex's funeral, a good friend took me away to the mountains.

My husband Phil returned to work, where he found purpose or distraction or both. We were not able to console one another very well, so I turned to others for support. Friends accompanied me on walks through Edmonton's river valley. Sometimes I would take my shoes off and walk in my bare feet, reconnecting with grass and soil, trying to regain my balance. But I felt so ungrounded.

One day, my cousin Glenda called and said, "You need to keep your eyes on the other side of the coulee." I grew up on the prairies, in southern Alberta, and as a child, I had encountered coulees: valleys with high, steep walls that can be dark, dangerous, and overgrown with vegetation. I found coulees scary and difficult to navigate. Could I get to "the other side" as Glenda advised? I began to try.

## STILL SUMMER 2012

*If you are going through hell, keep going.*
—Winston Churchill

I made a decision to seek professional help at Edmonton's Support Network, and attended one-on-one sessions with a suicide bereavement counsellor. Terri became a companion on my grief journey. I like this word, "companion." Grief is not an illness that needs to be cured by a therapist. It is a natural human reaction. But Terri explained that suicide often results in complicated grief and that trauma can ground itself in the body. How that presented for me was through panic attacks, anxiety, sleeplessness and hopelessness. Triggers for the panic attacks included: the sound of helicopters (the search for Alex included helicopters); crowds; news about missing people; and driving past the community where Alex had lived and died. I had suicide ideation. Once when I was in an upper floor stairwell I imagined jumping. I am so lucky I had someone with professional training to share my dark thoughts with.

I began to meditate and Terri offered me a mantra that was helpful:

*This is a moment of suffering*
*Suffering is a part of life*
*May I be kind to myself in this moment*
*May I give myself the compassion I need.*

Over the many months that I went to the Support Network, I worked hard to share my thoughts and feelings and follow guidance. One painful but illuminating exercise was to construct a personal trauma timeline. Terri walked me through my past, and over a number of sessions, she had me recount and depict other personal crises I'd experienced, such as my journey with breast cancer and the sudden death of my mother. This personal timeline review helped me to consider what had sustained me through hard times. My attitude started to vacillate between "no false strength" and "fake it until you make it."

At some point in the counselling process, I started to see the other side of the coulee and feel a bit of hope that I could create a new normal. I wanted to once again be a friend, sister, companion, and loving mother to my daughter. All of these identities had all but vanished, save the bereaved mother. My role as an artist had also disappeared. I had been an actor, a drama teacher, and a filmmaker. So, how to regain that creativity?

## FALL 2012

*How hard she worked at gathering the light.*
—Samantha Reynolds

When going through breast cancer I had been taught the importance of actively doing "hope work." I began creating a series of collages to visualize my hope, my expectation of better days ahead. I cut out photographs and words from magazines and cards, drew pictures, found relevant text, and pasted them into a scrapbook. These collages depicted what I wanted to see in my life—including images about improving my physical health and relationships with others, about beginning new creative projects, about doing advocacy work, and being in nature.

I did some gardening. Earlier in the year, my neighbour Kit and I, with the help of three of Alex's friends, had planted the Alex Garden. Given Alex's red hair, we planted anything that was orange or red, such as beets, carrots, and marigolds.

Our friends and neighbours gifted us with lilies that were also red and orange and yellow. Phil and I planted these in a garden bed that we could see from the living room window. Beside the plants we placed a paving stone embedded with a stained-glass snowboarder our friend Loraine had made for us.

So many other people found unique, creative ways to mourn and to express their grief over Alex's death. Phil chose a poem for a plaque, dedicated it to Alex, and gave it to the Youth Emergency Shelter along with a financial donation. Alex's workplace made a sculpture out of Alex's last weld, and also organized an Alex Thomas-Haug invitational golf tournament. I created a video scholarship for emerging filmmakers in his name. Friends painted

Alex's portrait; dedicated a video project to him; got tattoos of his initials ATH; made cards with the infinity symbol; made journals with a peregrine falcon on the cover (Alex had a tattoo of a falcon); adorned the bottom of Alex's snowboard with messages and drawings; made decals and pieces of temporary graffiti; and they wrote.

One precious gift of writing was from our Riverdale neighbour, Linda:

Alex's death broke our hearts. We are enduring that pain together and trying to make sense of all that happened. Have you asked yourself what that week of searching for him in May was all about, given the outcome? Was there any deeper purpose in the search, any point to it all? Here is a spark of possibility...

The search was love in action, not just love for Alex, but also love from him to the rest of us. Alex offered us an opportunity to see what matters in life, to perceive what is real and enduring, to grasp it and try to understand it. This transformative force of love in the community was his last gift to his family, and to his friends, and to the world. He brought people of all ages and backgrounds together in a single heartbeat: to search for him, to hope for him, and then to grieve for him, and to celebrate his fine character.... His true friends would have walked to the end of the earth to bring him home. In some ways that matter, you did bring him home. Alex will go with you, as he will stay with us.

Our daughter Cayley Thomas, an actor and musician, also wrote about Alex, producing her first album, *Ash Mountains,* and dedicating it to her brother. In performance, she would introduce these songs by talking about Alex; she encouraged audience members to be more communicative and to seek help if they were struggling. The first song she wrote was "Blue Summer."

barefoot *toes and hands in soil this* june

marigolds *and lilac trees in bloom*
they *left us milk and honey at our door*
afraid *we do not live there anymore*
summer *days are coming*
summer *days drag on*
it's *a blue, blue summer now you're gone*
sweet *perfume and sliver moon in* june
so *we run all lemon sun afternoon*
a *sultry breeze brings forth a sorry tune*
they *give and give but all I wish is you*
summer *days are coming*
summer *days drag on*
it's *a blue, blue summer now you're gone*

Soon after the release of this song, Cayley and I were invited
to participate in a photo-voice project organized by the School
of Nursing at the University of British Columbia. This research
project, "Man Up Against Suicide," raises awareness about male
suicide. The researchers send participants, like us, cameras, and
independently we take photos associated with our loss. When I
went out with the camera, I found I was still searching for Alex.
I went around Edmonton taking photos of where he had lived
and socialized. I also walked through my home and to the garage,
and I found and photographed objects that belonged to him.

One of my photos is of Alex's welding gloves and tool kit.
The researcher interviewed me about this photo, and she super-
imposed my words over the welding gloves: "They are seduced
by the promise of big money but are unprepared for the harsh
initiation." Through my work on the photography project, I
better understood how Alex, in order to make $60,000 a year,
had sacrificed his physical and mental health and ultimately his
life. One of Cayley's photos was of the prayer flags we draped
around the tree where Alex died. Her words: "I wish he would
have known the beauty of his life and the gaping hole that would
be left after his death."

The Man Up Against Suicide photo-voice exhibit has been
displayed in several cities across Canada, and there is a virtual
gallery online. This exhibit is helping others to talk about the

experience of being a loss survivor and is reducing the stigma and shame associated with mental health, substance use, and suicide.

### WINTER 2013

*Calling All Angels*
 Ten months after Alex died, we invited a group of twenty-five family members and friends to gather with Phil, Cayley, and me at Alex's favourite place—the mountains above Lake Louise. We rented rooms at the youth hostel, hosted a supper, and spent the evening socializing and sharing stories about our son. The next day, we took a gondola up the mountain as snow fell under blustery, cloudy skies.

As I looked down from the gondola, I could picture Alex sitting at the outdoor burger bar on the ski hill, laughing with his snowboard pals. I saw him standing in the parking lot, jumping on his friend for a piggyback ride. I saw him laughing as he waited in line for the chair lift, sporting a green toque, red gloves, baggy snowboard pants and jacket, and ski goggles. I saw him flying fifteen feet into the air after lifting off from a snowboard jump. Then he vanished as the gondola bumped me back to reality with an abrupt stop at the top of the mountain.

The sun came out, and under a brilliant blue sky, we stood in a circle scattering Alex's ashes in the snow and throwing handfuls of coloured powder on top. We read poems, chanted together, and cried. We fanned out, and each person found a special spot to lie down in the snow and make a snow angel.

I had invited our Facebook friends to join us vicariously that day. More than 250 people around the world made snow angels, or sand angels, or air angels in memory of Alex. They sent us the photos of their angels, along with memories. I so wanted people to remember Alex's short but important life, and that was happening. Joy started to find its way into my broken heart.

### MAY 2013

*Ambassadors for Alex*
 On the first anniversary of Alex's passing, I began in earnest my

advocacy work around suicide prevention, mental health promotion, and education around substance use. I had begun this effort within days after he died. Fearful that his suicide would trigger self-harm by his peers or others in our community, a phenomenon known as contagion, I gathered and distributed literature about suicide prevention. But because of my poor health, it wasn't until a year later that I could continue this advocacy work.

Our family invited people from the community to a public gathering. One hundred friends and family members attended. My main message was to encourage people to envision the unimaginable. Most people, upon hearing that our son had died by suicide, had said, "I can't imagine it." As my friend Anne wrote, "Most of us cannot even get near this thought of a family member taking their life. It is like approaching a fire or something ... you can't make yourself do it." But at our Ambassadors for Alex gathering, I asked people to face the fact that everyone is vulnerable to suicide, particularly when they experience loss, including a loss of hope. My presentation concluded with some facts and strategies:

> People who contemplate suicide have often struggled long and hard, putting up valiant battles with incredible pain. Sometimes suicide is an impulsive act. Ask the person. Are you thinking of harming yourself or taking your life? Do you have a plan? Assure them that you will listen and are a safe person to talk to; offer to accompany the person to a doctor or a walk-in mental health clinic. If the person is a danger to himself, call the mental health crisis line.

After the presentation, our family distributed packages of literature on mental illness, substance use and suicide awareness. We asked people to be Ambassadors for Alex by sharing this knowledge with others.

The evening ended with the distribution of colourful pens and lanterns. We wrote messages to Alex on large sky lanterns. We went outside, lit the wicks, and when they filled with hot air, we released the fifty orange lanterns. As they drifted upward we laughed and cheered and watched them disappear into the evening sky.

## TODAY

*Instead of asking why they left, now I ask what beauty
will I create in the space they no longer occupy?*
—Rudy Facisco

The tragedy of Alex's suicide and my reaction to that reality changed my life irrevocably. But my compulsion to know the why behind my son's death has waned. I have made it to the other side of the coulee and am engaged with life again. I have co-founded a group called Moms Stop The Harm—a network of Canadian mothers and families whose loved ones have died because of substance use or who hope for recovery. I have joined a choir and learned to play the ukulele. I can laugh again and share stories about my son's beautiful twenty-four years of life. I am really proud of who Alex was, what he accomplished, and how much love he gave to his friends and family and community. I do not want to let him go, or say goodbye. I have not lost him. I experience many precious moments when a star, sunrise, flower, bird, fox, or butterfly triggers a feeling of togetherness with Alex. It is my son saying hello.

Recently, a young friend asked if there was a special place where he could go to remember or pay homage to our son. That gave us the idea to dedicate a memorial bench to Alex and to have it in our community. The bench is located on the eastern edge of our Edmonton neighbourhood of Riverdale, and it overlooks the North Saskatchewan River. The plaque on the bench reads "Alex Thomas Haug. 1987–2012. Forever in Our Hearts." There is also an infinity sign and the words "Big Love,"—a phrase that he used when saying goodbye or signing off on an email or text. I go to the bench often. As I sit on Alex's bench, I remember that his eyes were as blue as the sky, his hair was as red as the sunset, and his love was as expansive as the river. And I feel deeply that I will always be Alexander's mother.

# 5.
# Crash

LISA WHITESIDE

THE DEATH OF MY BEAUTIFUL and kind-hearted daughter still cripples me today. It's been two and a half years, but the pain is still so deep, and the tears continue to flow.

My daughter died in a car crash outside of Edson, Alberta, on a moonless night at approximately 2:00 a.m. She was twenty-two years old.

I got a phone call from my older daughter Krista in the early morning hours of 23 January 2014. All she said was "Mum, Lexi's dead." Then she told me the details. I guess my initial reaction was shock and disbelief, but that was very quickly replaced by incredible emotional pain and grief—the depths of which I had never felt before.

I couldn't believe it: my baby was gone!

I've cried so many tears and continue to cry. Not every day now, but my tears still flow. I miss her so much.

A part of me died with her. I will continue to survive, but there will always be a hole in my soul.

# 6.
# Alessandra

DONNA MCCART SHARKEY

WE SPENT THE SUMMER of her fourteenth year and her sister's ninth at a house beside the Lake of Two Mountains in Québec. It was a soothing place and Alessandra loved it dearly. She walked with our Weimaraner six, seven, sometimes eight hours each day exploring the shore of the lake. Five months after she died, I returned there. Standing on the wharf, the wind blew back some of her ashes as I was placing them into the water and they landed on my fleece sweater. How like her, I thought, ever wanting to be close.

I released more of her ashes into the Atlantic Ocean at Trinity East, Newfoundland, then some into the Pacific near Victoria, more into the Ottawa River, in a small pond near our home, and in a wooded area near a friend's home in rural Québec. In June, I planted a low bush cranberry near the ocean in Newfoundland. The arborist who sold it to me said, "it will last a long time. It's a sturdy tree." Yes, like my daughter, always sturdy. Her spirit, sturdy too. She had beaten so many odds that it appeared she would keep on. At least that's what I had believed before.

My daughter Alessandra died during the night of 16 November 2013, by herself, in a room in a hospital psychiatric unit. When a nurse did rounds at 2:30 a.m., she called Code Blue. For thirty-five minutes, they tried to restart her heart. It never did.

For a long time before she died, time and time again, I pushed down my fear. Just fear, I told myself. She's strong. She had already survived so much; she had to prevail. Five months before her death, she stopped breathing, and was resuscitated. Three months, then again two months, before she died, the same thing occurred. The morning before she died, her heart stopped again. Still I couldn't let myself believe—out of fear, not knowing, and not knowing what to do.

But on high alert, vigilant, I always kept my phone beside my bed at night. Just in case. Crises had happened, and I panicked each time a call came in the night, an emergency. From Alessandra, from a friend of hers, or from a hospital saying, "She's here. She's in intensive care. In a coma. Come now."

I knew another emergency call would come. But how could I have known this, this call?

The phone screams within inches of my ear, and I know. Still in semi-sleep, before I even say a desperate hello into the mouthpiece, I know. Something is different this time. Shaking, I leap from my bed. I need to stand up. It's 3:30 a.m.

The nurse starts by telling me about Alessandra's day. She went to her brother's place, and then she returned to the hospital for dinner—shepherd's pie, rice pudding. During the evening, she joked and chatted with some people. She told Jennifer, another patient, that she liked her new red shoes and that she had always wanted a pair of red shoes just like hers. She watched television and went to bed at 10:00 p.m.

I grip the phone even harder. Why is the nurse telling me about my daughter's day? Wake up, I tell myself. What's happening? I want her to hurry up. Is there a reason for her to be telling me this? Then, as she says the words, "I was doing my rounds and got to her room at the far end of the hall," I feel like I have been punched in the throat, and I wake up hard. Enough. "Is she dead?" I scream. I hear my scream, but it sounds like someone else's voice. In the pitch black of the room, I start shivering.

"We tried" she says. "We tried for thirty-five minutes." I barely hear her describe how they tried, how many were there, all trying. I ask, still standing in the dark, "What do I do now? Should I come to the hospital?"

"No," she says. "Wait until the morning. Your daughter will still be in her bed. Drink a glass of water." But I know I can't wait until the morning. She says "I'm sorry." We hang up.

My heart is pounding against my chest wall, pounding with

shock, pounding death hard, frantic in this after-death, in this hardly real life. I feel out of my body, somewhere else, but not in my body. My brain is taut, as though in a vice, and tries to make sense of the impossible, the impossible that is stunning me, searing me.

The house feels cold. My body sags as I walk downstairs. In the kitchen, I make a cup of tea. I turn on my computer hoping to find out that what I had just heard was incorrect. Perhaps someone has emailed me to tell me the nurse was mistaken. Maybe someone wrote "I'm with her right now. Don't worry." But no one had.

I wander into the living room and stare out the window at the moonless November night, the world emptied. I need to tell someone. Say the words. But in the middle of the night? I call a dear friend two provinces over. She tells me she'll come as soon as she can; hopefully, she'll get a flight that day. I start to get dressed to go to the hospital, but my mind is jumping wildly. I pull out all my sweaters from my closet. They land on the floor of my bedroom, scattered, looking in disrepair.

Somehow I get to the hospital, to her room. The intubation tube is still in her mouth, with tape along her cheeks holding the tube in place; her face is turned toward the window, full of night. Emergency equipment has been left beside her. I look at the EKG grid paper showing her heartbeat. All the lines are flat. I look at her, stilled. I hold her hand in mine, stroke her head, and weep. This is my daughter. Now dead.

When I return home, I wait for her sister Renata, who is driving back from Toronto. She bounces into the house happy and excited to tell me about her trip. But I stop her and say, "Come, come upstairs." "What is it" she asks, looking worried, her smile now gone. We sit on my bed and somehow the words come out of my mouth. "Your sister died." She looks at me, stunned. We both cry. She says, "Oh mum, I feel sorry for you." I say back to her, "And I feel sorry for you." We both deeply mean it. Our family of three, now two.

Renata and I go to the hospital. This time it is daylight and a guard stands at Alessandra's door. A pair of red shoes lies on the floor outside her room. Renata picks them up, and we find Jennifer, the young woman who owns the shoes. She knows Alessandra died in the night; she tells us she wants the shoes to go to her. With thanks, Renata returns them to Jennifer. "You wear them," she says, "they'll look beautiful on you." The red shoes Alessandra almost got.

Inside her room, the emergency equipment has been removed. We stay until it's time to leave, time for the last hug, the last time to hold her hand. But I don't know how to never see her again—to walk out of her room and to say goodbye. I tell myself this: walk to the door of the room. Open it. Look straight ahead. Keep walking down the hall. Into the elevator. Then the car. And I repeat to myself. Don't cry now. Don't cry.

We bring all of Alessandra's belongings home in two green garbage bags: her clothes, wallet, a ring, watch, cell phone, her glasses, books. At home, I open her wallet—six dollars and ten cents. Her money. All of it.

It was confusing at first. Some people said, "You'll get over it." Others said, "You're never the same person again." For me, this was my experience: I got over a long winter cold after my daughter died. I got over a cold sore after the cold. After that, a long season pulled me into terrible darkness. During that time, reading and writing were the places I went to. I read about death and grief and I started a journal of sorts—writing words to recall her voice, the feeling of her hand in mine, her hilarious comments and unique approach to life, to this world. All the memories I feared forgetting. I wrote to myself and often I wrote to her. I still do.

Dear Alessandra,

Your dreams fell apart one by one. My dreams for you also fell apart. Your adolescence and your twenties were marred by difficulties: suicide attempts, self-harm, and the emergence of mental illness. Hospital admissions disrupted your schooling, friendships, your sense of yourself, your confidence in your future. Group homes were fraught with long waitlists. At times, medications produced egregious side-effects. I was sorry for you.

When you died, I felt like I'd never be happy.

But I should have known

that for a long time I had been mourning your torn potential, mourning your mental illness, your health, your energetic self no longer bicycling, rollerblading, playing basketball, running with our dog.

Mourning your paraplegia, your back broken from a suicide attempt off your apartment balcony, always mourning.

My grief, before you died, after you died, was contained each time within a shock, hearing these words: suicide attempt, homeless shelter, another shelter, then another, another suicide attempt, another. Dead.

I should have known

that your heart would stop and not start again one of the times, any time, maybe soon. But no, I thought your heart would always start again.

Dear Alessandra,
I apologize

that I was grumpy the last day you were at my home five days before your death. You were always so forgiving. Thank you. Renata was braiding your hair, and we had lunch and later coffee. I listened to your quirky stories, which I always loved. You left with your boyfriend. I could have been less grumpy, cheery even. If only I had known.

That day, the last time I saw you—no, not the last time I saw you, the last time I saw you alive, vibrant, smiling—you waved goodbye to me as you rolled down the wheelchair ramp in front of the house. At the bottom of the ramp, you hugged me, gave me a big kiss on my cheek and said, "See you soon. I'll come for dinner on Saturday." As you passed me, you turned and blew me a kiss with your hand. "Bye," you sang, as you rode off. The sun was setting behind you, and made you glow almost gold in the sumptuous autumn light. You were happy, immensely loving life that day in a way I can only aim toward.

But wait, a week before, I saw an ad in the newspaper for a newly opened cooperative funeral home. I cut out the ad, not thinking why. No reason. I left it on the edge of my bookcase where it stayed until decisions had to be made. I still wonder why I cut it out—the entangled knowing and not knowing.

Why didn't I

spend more time with you? Why didn't I have breakfast with you the last morning before you died? You called to ask me to meet you at Rockin' Johnny's, your favourite breakfast place. Always with the same waitress, Betty. Always for you fried eggs and sausages, white toast, black coffee. Me, poached, brown toast, coffee with milk. But that morning I said no.

But still, the shock when the phone rang, the night after I didn't meet you for breakfast.

Then,

two weeks after you died, I drove past you standing on a street corner. I was sure it was you, so I drove around the block back to that corner. When I got back there, no one was there.

A month later, at the ocean's edge at loud high tide, I called your name into and beyond the waves, calling you loud and long, fervently hoping you would hear me, hoping you were there.

It was a long time before I could face the memories of us walking the dog on summer evenings—swimming, laughing, hiking, dancing, singing. The desolation and the wanting you back was that visceral.

Dear Alessandra,
I should have known

that I would get a phone call. But instead, I aimed toward life.

You probably know

that I joined a bereaved families group because I knew I had to face my grief directly. Going to the first meeting was terrifying for me. But the group, all with this shared experience and shell shocked still, proved to be an anchor; this group was one none of us ever thought we would be part of before we absolutely needed to.

And you probably know this too

that I found it hard, making a person uncomfortable by crying, showing the pain, that dreadful sinkhole that no one wants to look into, to imagine for themselves. I say "I'm so sorry. I didn't mean to cry." Making someone witness this, someone who piled up her courage to say the words and this is what I give back—tears.

And this

that I'd be asked the question. I meet some people for the first time shortly after you died, and they talk about their children. I sit in frozen fear as one of them turns to me and says, "Do you have children? How many do you have?" I stumble my way through the answer, and hold my arms tight across my stomach.

Dear Alessandra,
I spend half of the next year close to the ocean on Bonavista Peninsula in Newfoundland. I need the ocean, the ruggedness, the rural air to breathe. I watch the waves of the North Atlantic, the whales, the artist's sky, eagles, the myriad stars, the moon. They nurture me.

After a year, the coroner's report arrives. I'm hopeful to end the not knowing and to learn the reason you died. But the report states that the coroner was unable to ascertain the cause of your death.

Dear Alessandra,
I tell you this

for a year, your death makes me a too cautious driver, nervous I won't see what's in front of me. Afraid someone might die, another driver, a biker, a walker, a rogue child. At times, this caution makes me forget where I'm going, how to get there.

And also

The isolation I imposed on myself during the year was because large groups were too wearing.

I should have known

that your future may have been bleak—painful bed sores making an infectious route through your body, effects of diabetes, arthritic pain, suicide. I'll leave it there. Still, not conciliatory.

I know this

Over two years later, I still carefully watch over my emotions.
Sometimes unexpectedly I get overwhelmed. I have days when exhaustion lays me low.
I never got over your death like that winter cold. There is no fast fix. No, I continue on—sometimes with joy, laughter, even hilarity, good experiences, and sometimes with a sadness weighing heavily on my chest. I avoid sad movies. I cry easily. At just about anything. I've never stopped yearning to see you.

I say this to you

When people mention you, a memory of an event, something you said, I light up. "Thank you," I say.

Dear Alessandra,
I know you understand why I say that I still can't hear the song, "I'm Leaving on a Jet Plane," without crying.
It's now almost three years later. I think about you every day. I read the obits in the newspaper. I want to hold you, hear you tell me a joke, meet you again at your favourite breakfast restaurant. Buy you a pair of red shoes.

I wish you had owned a pair of red shoes.

I have regrets

that I couldn't prevent your death

that you will never see your sister's new first house, my new dog, Bobby.

Dear Alessandra,
 I want you to know this

That each time I write to you, even now, I cry. And yesterday, two months exactly before the third anniversary of your death, my crying turned into uncontrollable sobbing, my body re-feeling the experience of hearing that you had died. And a day later, today, with anguish and anxiety still covering me, a sensation of unreality holds onto me, brings me almost to a standstill, and makes this writing even more difficult.

 But this, too

 that people have supported me with tea, dinners, phone calls, visits, listening, and caring. I hold their courage and love firmly in my heart. Without everyone, my pain would have seared longer, more achingly.

 But still

 I have made slow, tentative changes, sometimes barely noticed. The despair is less deep now and my awareness of life and nature more profound. Knowing that our bodies and minds can hold so much suffering, I treasure sunsets even more than ever. That kindness and small things matter, really matter, make the present vastly important.

 And there's more.

 One day recently, I made an assumption that you would want me to be happy—an assumption, but I'll go with it anyway—that perhaps this is the best way, though hard, to show how much I love you.

And most importantly, I need you to know this

The world does appear slightly safer to me now. Less unpredictability courses through my daily thoughts, and true or not, it's a better feeling. I'm no longer fearful of driving my car. My brain has come back to itself, as has my energy. I'm less tethered to pain. But some things stay the same, and mostly this. You, Alessandra, with your big and extroverted spirit, you're with me in my heart every day. And will be.

# 7.
# Airborne

MARTHA ROYEA

I'LL START AT THE END with a paragraph from my son's obituary:

> Rick has been loved deeply, faithfully, and patiently through years of turbulence and times of joyful stability. There are things that love can't overcome. Like all addicts, Rick tried again and again to free himself from the substances he leaned on, but always that greater hunger, wordless and insistent, hounded him until it ha its way. This is the burden Rick came in with and that crushed him in the end. We knew the good and generous man beneath that struggle. We miss him. We thank him for coming into this world; we open our hearts to his sweet release.

It's three years since my son died. Sometimes when I light the nightly candle I look at his picture on the mantel and I don't believe he's gone. I think *Rick hasn't called for a while*. I think *one of these days the phone will ring*. I think *if anything was wrong, I'd know, I'd feel it*. And then I remember: *he's OK now. He's just fine*.

All that's left is what memory can round up through old photographs, letters, the brief, enigmatic emails he sent me from time to time. Certain gestures, words and phrases, sounds and smells. And the images that spring up in my head when I think of him—*how fiercely you battled and butted your way out of my body into the too-bright air, and how you would have flown then if you could.*

How many mothers have lost their sons to flight of one kind or another? Those adventurous boys, the reckless, the thoughtless, the ones who crave and whose craving can never be satisfied, not by money and materials, not by success, not by pleasure, and not by love. Those restless ones who seek out distance and the edges of danger, whose friends say of them, "He must have a death wish."

On 6 June 2013, the man who was my son, beloved stranger, died at around four o'clock in the afternoon slumped over a kitchen table, face down on the powdery surface, a plastic drinking straw still up his nose: heroin, the way he preferred it. He had been drinking and using steadily for days. His face was swollen and bruised. One by one, his housemates came home from work or school, saw him slumped over the table and walked on to their respective rooms; evidently, it wasn't an unusual sight. It may have been a couple of hours before one of them remarked that he hadn't moved at all and went to see if he was breathing. He wasn't. My boy was fifty, hardly a child, but still a child, my child. My only son.

Five years earlier, in 2008—when his wife had finally given up on him and left and he was deep in his silent sorrow, alone and snowed in with his menagerie of animals in the hills outside Santa Fe—I wrote this poem. I didn't send it to him then. I can't remember why, only that I knew this was a dark time for him, that it would be deeper and more treacherous than any previous one because he had lost his beloved Juli now, and was about to lose everything else as well. Dread began to overtake me: this time he might not be able to "battle and butt his way" into the light, as he had done so many times before.

### SON IN WINTER

It's Christmas. I see you
sprawled in the middle of a sofa
you have all to yourself.
The TV is on and you're looking
through half-closed eyes at your hands
lolling empty, palms up on your thighs.

It's Christmas. But what does that mean?
Not even the dogs come near you,
and your best friend rolls around

empty on the coffee table
between a messy stack of motorcycle magazines
and the hardening remains of the last time you ate.
Love is a long way off.
The road is nowhere visible.

It's Christmas. I see you
alone,
the sky falling
all around you,
white,
silent,
cold.

On the day he died, Rick prepared a meal on a tray and took it into his lair. He had been living in Baltimore for three years by then. He had a job he liked and a relationship he didn't but couldn't seem to leave. He'd had several close calls with death. He had spent times sober and productive, times bingeing and time in jail for driving under the influence. That day, he chose a DVD and placed it in the slot on the TV. He plumped his pillows and turned down the bed covers, opened a can of beer, and put the rest of the six-pack on the floor beside the bed. Clearly he had a plan. Surely it wasn't to end his life.

Police labelled cause of death simply "overdose." They didn't use the word "accidental." They didn't mention suicide. Everyone who knew Rick rejected that idea. Not that that he wasn't suicidal at times, but an overdose would not have been his way out and a home he shared with others wouldn't have been the place. That last snort at the kitchen table was surely just part of what had become his ritual preparation for another evening of romancing oblivion. Or was it?

I have had frequent flashes of scenes from that 1995 Nicolas Cage film *Leaving Las Vegas*, like the one where someone suggests that Cage's drinking is a way to kill himself, and he responds: "Killing myself is a way to drink." Flippant. But still, at some point that vicious circularity has its own irresistible momentum. Is that where Rick was?

And does it matter, the manner of death? Does it make a difference to grief? Long before my son died, grief had come to make a nest in my heart. It took the form of guilt—that it was my failure as a mother that caused his unhappiness, his need to escape into booze and danger. It took the form of anger that he blamed me just as much as I blamed myself; he refused to take responsibility for his own choices and actions. It took the form of fear over and over again throughout the years of his adulthood. Would he kill himself on one of his motorcycles, in one of his cars? Would he kill someone else with his reckless driving? Would he fall into traffic, get beaten up by thugs, or get "done" by some drug baron? And it took the form of hope every time he pulled the pieces of his life back together for a while, rebuilt his broken bridges, and regained some of his self-respect. It was a tenuous hope, a hope against hope, each time more hesitant, some part of me braced for the phone call that I knew would come. The last phone call. And when it did, what sailed in on the flood tide of emotion and disorientation was relief, like being able to exhale after a long-held breath. My son was free. And so was I—freed from the fear of loss into loss itself, into the grace that is letting go.

This story will never be finished. There is no end to love. That which tethers our hearts to those wondrous beings our bodies bring forth into this world, that tends them and tries to protect them, helps them stand and steadies them when they fall, dreams their success, wishes their happiness, frets and doubts and falters and celebrates and sometimes loses them—that love, unleashed from all those earthly concerns, can expand in a greater space.

In the first days after Rick's death, I kept a candle burning day and night. *Come home*, I begged silently. *Come home. We'll start again. It will be better, I promise.* And then there he was swimming in the air a little above my head, laughing, "It's OK Mum. Don't worry so much about me. It's all good. It's all good." And I knew that for him, it was.

# 8.
# Something I Want You to Know

MARTHA ROYEA

*For my son, 1963 – 2013*

The night of your conception was a friendly night,
a night of many moons and a star.

A motorcycle stood silhouetted on a hill.
Someone bayed like a wolf. A Porsche, unmistakable,
streaked across the sky. On the night of your conception

there were candles in a forest; cats staring out of shadows,
dogs sniffing the air for news of you. They already knew their names.

Hidden in undergrowth, a book that would open all books,
a girl named after a flower, a girl named after an opera, a girl
who had once been a boy. And the one girl.

That night a banana tree grew through the middle of the house.
Tins of tuna, jars of peanut butter, loaves of Wonder Bread,
Cheez Whiz, Ritz Crackers, Wagon Wheels, began to stake out
their shelf space in the dark behind last year's preserves.

The rooms filled with phantoms—car parts, bike handles, gizmos,
and contraptions only you would know the names of.

It was mild. It was May.
All that had been tense and fearful

fled into the dank earth deep beneath the house,
slouched there hatching plans, biding time.

But the night of your conception, that was a good night,
a peaceful night. It was May. Languid and oblivious

they turned to each other in sleep, your father, your mother.
A motorcycle idled on a hill. Someone bayed like a wolf.

*Ohh!* you must have said,
and your sister in her crib, eyes wide in the dark: *Ohh!*

# 9.
# Ten Days Apart

JACQUELYN JOHNSTON

SOMETIMES PEOPLE SAY TO ME "I can't imagine what you're going through." And I think, "Neither can I. What if your two children died ten days apart in separate accidents? How would you feel? I can't imagine how you'd feel, or how I do."

The shock that dropped like a glacier flung at high speed through the cosmos landed on my chest and stole my breath. It sat there, sits there, slowly melting, my tears its run-off. Twenty months after I received the news that my beautiful twenty-two-year-old daughter Shiloh was hit by a car and killed on the sidewalk on her lunch break, I am still in shock.

Actually, it was the aftershock from a week and a half before when I found my darling twenty-year-old daughter Keziah in still repose, forever sleeping on the floor of her apartment, the result of an accidental overdose of heroin and cocaine. Her death meant the fear of her dying after a four-year battle with drug addiction (primarily heroin) was over.

I never really thought it would happen. I had already lost my little boy, Emmanuel, to asphyxiation in his crib at twenty-two and a half months twenty-six years before. Surely I wouldn't be the unlucky recipient of a second lost child. Surely one of her attempts at recovery would be successful. But it was not to be. The rollercoaster stopped on its tracks mid-ride, and made me the bereaved mother of two—a distinction I held for a mere ten days before the personal death toll climbed to three. All my children.

It was absolutely impossible for me to figure out what to think about this or how to comprehend it. Besides the enormity of losing all my children, the proximity of Shiloh and Keziah's deaths was mind blowing. I've heard that to survive suffering, one must derive some meaning from it.

But I couldn't figure out what it could mean or why it should have happened. Am I supposed to learn something from this, and if so, couldn't it be taught some other way? What am I supposed to learn? What on earth? I have no idea. It makes no sense. It just seems bizarre, a random cruel fate. Why me? Why them? Why? Around my head the questions swirled, going nowhere.

The overwhelming, generous outpouring of expressions of sympathy underlined for me that this was a very, very bad thing that had happened, so bad that strangers were compelled to commiserate. A church and light refreshments were donated to accommodate the more than nine hundred attendees at the memorial service. Cards, donations, pictures, and time were all freely given.

Somehow the media had caught the story, which made it feel like the whole world knew my business. I felt as though my wretched life was on display, and I didn't know who had seen the news. I felt like I had to be good all the time and to behave in ways befitting a grieving mother, but not an angry one or a swearing one or even a dancing one.

It didn't seem right to publicly enjoy my life, even though the shock sometimes allowed that. I like to do my emoting at home. I prefer to keep my composure in public, but even that seemed to carry judgment in my mind that I didn't seem sad enough.

The fact is that I avoid the pain when I can and succumb when I can't. I don't feel as if I've really grieved properly, or enough yet. It's been twenty months since the girls died. When Emmanuel died, I howled inhumanly.

I'm afraid of drowning in the pain. It's like a fiery inferno, like liquid hell, at the bottom of a huge precipice. As I near the edge, I feel the heat. I release some tears that wet me enough to keep me from crisping, and I back away. I just can't go there all the way yet. I'm writing my memoir, and I can talk and write the story dry eyed. As long as I tell the story, I approach the edge without feeling the pain, but when I feel the story, I plunge into the abyss and am consumed, or so I imagine.

The biggest part of grief I've struggled with is guilt. Logically, I recognize it's a normal part of grief. I've noticed that often when someone dies, some people blame themselves and some people blame others. I blame myself. I was not directly responsible for any of my children's deaths, but indirectly ... that is a meandering path into the forest that will lead you to the candy-coated house of the old witch, who will try to kill you with a boiling pot of recriminations. Oh wait, wrong fairy tale—a hot oven of recriminations.

I wish I'd been a better mother. Unfortunately, because of an undiagnosed mood disorder my parenting wasn't all it should have been. Regret is like sandpaper that keeps my heart sore and raw. I know my children loved me and vice versa. That love lives on. That is the exquisite beauty and mystery of human relationships: we live in each other's hearts, minds, and memories.

For me, the challenge is to cling to the good and blow the chaff away. It seems to keep blowing back in my face.

This brings me to another troubling aspect of being a bereaved mother. Where did my children go? Where does the wind blow? No one knows. But I am compelled to come to some decision about my beliefs regarding their destination. Whenever I move, my mother comes for a visit so she can picture where I am when we're talking on the phone five hundred miles apart. Mothers need to know where their children are.

The night I received the news that Shiloh had been killed, I was in Mexico at a writing retreat. It took my sister five days searching for me and getting to Mexico to deliver to me in person the awful news. My trip had been booked before Keziah died, and even though it was guilt inducing, my family all encouraged me to go, which allowed me some time and space to grieve quietly. We postponed Keziah's funeral service until I got back. Even Shiloh encouraged me to go; she said that she would take care of organizing her sister's service. And I knew that writing is healing.

I went out onto the lighted balcony of my hotel room to sit with the information and my journal. I looked up to see, framed by palm trees, two stars, the only two I could see in the sky, one bigger than the other. I thought *what if we become stars when we die*? I can just imagine the girls saying, "Let's go to mom and see if she notices us." Twinkling to a star is like waving to a human.

The only thing about my theory that may be right is the number of human souls that have died throughout history may equal the billions of stars. But I don't really believe that's what happens. Being raised as a Protestant Christian, I am inclined to believe in heaven, but my notions are vague. The Bible doesn't offer much description of the place. What do people do there? What would my kids do there?

I spent a lot of time during my bereavement leave from work googling theories about life after death. Some people believe that the spirit is eternal, and returns to earth in many incarnations for the purpose of spiritual growth, or that we all have spiritual guides and the ones we lose become our helpers on the other side. Some believe our guides help us choose an incarnation to best help us on our journey, including choosing our parents. Supposedly, aborted children (of which I've had three) are ones that realize they aren't ready to come back or it isn't a good time. I don't know about that.

However, I found it interesting and comforting to explore different beliefs, which are really just stories we tell ourselves to feel better; they enable us to cope with our situations and fear of the unknown. I've decided that my children are living lives in another dimension and that we are still connected in our hearts and minds telepathically. I talk to them sometimes, but I don't expect an answer. I've asked for signs but didn't get them.

I've interpreted naturally occurring events as being signs from them, and I've drawn comfort from them. For example, the day after I heard that Shiloh was dead, I was walking over to the writing retreat leader's place with a friend, and I noticed a small, bare-branched tree with two butterflies dancing among the branches. As I approached, they both stopped for a moment so I could look closely at them and then continued their dance. One was yellow, Shiloh's favourite colour. As we continued to walk, my friend casually said, "Oh, look at those pretty flowers." I glanced at the empty lot filled with yellow and purple flowers. Shiloh's boyfriend had been planning to propose to her the following month on their anniversary. Their wedding colours were to be purple and yellow. Often when I see two of something, like two flocks of birds swooping low overhead, it reminds me of my daughters. We all have to find ways to comfort ourselves, I think, and we get to choose how to do that.

Being diagnosed with bipolar disorder at the age of forty-seven was actually a relief because it finally offered an explanation for some otherwise dubious behaviour. It gave me an opportunity to try and forgive myself for some bad parenting. My doctor said it wasn't my fault and told my girls that. Now that I am medicated, it's both a blessing and a curse. My mood-stabilizing drugs prevent me from plummeting into the abyss, but they also prevent me from experiencing the refining power of deep suffering. Oops, there's that old Christianity rising up again. Never mind.

In the past, I used stand-up comedy as a therapeutic means of dealing with dark times, such as when my husband and I split up. Humour, like writing, is healing. The only joke I can think of so far about this situation is that I want to put some of those family stickers on my rear-car window, but I can't find a mom and three caskets. Nope, not funny. Still sad. Too soon?

Each of my children brought unique gifts into my life. Emmanuel brought joy and purpose. Shiloh was my delight (her middle name); she was articulate, talented, and kind to all, while Keziah amazed me with her persistence, original wit, beauty, and style. I have no one to help me with the computer or cell phone anymore or keep me up to date on the latest fashion trends and expressions. I've lost my second and third opinions of possible outfits.

But more than that, my loss is enormous. The reminders of them are everywhere, daily. I wear clothing and jewellery that the girls gave me as gifts. My eyes sting every time I enter a Starbucks. It was a regular hangout place for us. When Shiloh was working at an art studio she visited so often and tipped so well the staff came to the memorial service. Every drive-thru and restaurant we ate at pangs. Every time I see something in a store I know they'd love, I ache. And it's not just the things that are around, it's the things that aren't—grandchildren. Conversations abound among women my age about their beloved grandchildren. I don't live in self-pity, but I do feel a certain wistfulness sometimes.

I'm grateful for the time I had with them and for their love and for all they taught me. My love for them is as deep as my pain.

# 10.
# Kevin

ROY PATTERSON

## LETTER TO MY SON

Kevin,

I wish you were still here.

I miss you every day.

I think about you every day.

There is always something I see or do that reminds me of you.

I miss joking around with you.

I miss picking you up from work and finding out how your day was.

I miss going to movies with you.

I miss your big bear hugs.

All of your family and friends really miss you. Mike and Josh are really hurting.

Zipper sleeps on your bed now—I'm sure he thinks you'll be back sometime.

I wish you had been more careful and not used a drug that was so dangerous. Did you really think you could beat the odds that many times? I should be angry with you, but I realize what severe anxiety and addiction did to you. You weren't thinking straight. I wish you had listened to me though and stopped using fentanyl. You were playing with your life and lost.

You used to be anxious and depressed but you didn't realize the positive impact you had on so many lives. We heard so many positive comments from your friends and co-workers. If you had heard some of those when you were alive perhaps you would have had more confidence in yourself and not thought you needed drugs and alcohol to survive.

I miss you and will always love you.
Love, Dad XOX

## LETTER FROM MY SON KEVIN

Dad,
I wish I were still there with you, Mom, and Zipper.
I miss you and think about you everyday also.
I miss joking around with you also, Putz.
I miss all of the things we used to do together.
I also miss everyone else. I really miss Mike and seeing Benjamin grow up.

I knew fentanyl was dangerous, but I didn't think it would kill me. As usual you and Mom were right, but you know I never listened very closely to what you said about addiction and had to learn for myself. Unfortunately, I learned too late.

I'm glad you're not angry with me. I never liked it when you got angry with me and stopped talking. It was good when we made up and hugged. I could use a hug right now.

Glad to hear people were saying nice things about me. I had a good family and lots of friends. Say hello to everyone for me and give Zipper a big hug for me.

I'm sorry I put you and Mom through all of the pain with my addictions. I didn't mean to cause you pain.

I'm not anxious or depressed anymore Dad.
I miss you and will always love you too!
Love, Kevin XOX

## EULOGY FOR MY SON

Kevin came into the world with a bang. We checked into the Ottawa Civic Hospital maternity ward at 11:30 p.m. on 4 October 1985. The doctor ball-parked that Kevin would be born seven or eight hours later. Well, Kevin had his own plans. He was born an hour and three quarters later at 1:15 a.m. on 5 October.

He was a busy baby and an active, happy toddler. At two years old, Jane found Kevin gleefully splashing in the toilet as if it were his own water park. She grabbed a camera and got a great candid shot of this moment of pure joy. Jane's mom, Rita, was so proud that Jane stayed in the moment and grabbed the camera instead of freaking out about germs.

In hindsight, there were many indications that Kevin had some sort of anxiety disorder. For the first three years of school, the teachers had to peel him off Jane before she could leave. Once she was gone, he made friends and worked well.

His teachers always reported that he was polite and did his work. This was important to us because courtesy, honesty, and taking pride in one's work are traits that we value and tried to instill in our children. Kevin was a good speller, and math came easily to him. In art, though, Kevin was a minimalist. If he could squiggle two lines down the page and pass it off as complete, he would.

Kevin didn't get into trouble in elementary school very often. When he did, it usually involved someone being bullied and Kevin intervening on their behalf. That was Kevin from an early age. He could not see a person in trouble and walk away.

Kevin and Ryan were the best of brothers. They hardly ever fought growing up and were still close even through the issues that sometimes arose throughout years of addiction.

Kevin had a group of friends who all grew up together in Kanata and always stayed friends: Mike, Matt, Josh, Phil, Tom, Lee, Rob, and many more. I know they all miss Kevin.

Kevin made friends easily. He didn't think he did, but you could see how people seemed at ease with him once he started talking to them.

But Kevin was racked with severe anxiety. He was never comfortable in most situations and was anxious around people—they didn't understand how a guy six foot five inches tall and three hundred pounds could be anxious. He was! He was so anxious that some days he would not even stand in the doorway of our garage to have a smoke; he would only walk down our street late at night when he knew no one would be there. That is why he turned to drugs and alcohol—to ease anxiety and try and fit in.

Yes, Kevin was a large imposing man, but he was a big teddy bear. He loved kids and animals, especially our cat Zipper, and was always looking out for his friends. He didn't have a violent bone in his body. He loved a good joke and would talk your ear off if he was having a good day.

I think Kevin would have been a great father. When I watched him play with Mike's son Benjamin, his godson, they seemed like two little kids playing—one just bigger than the other.

Kevin had just turned thirty years old recently. I just turned sixty last week. He and I were very similar in a lot of ways:

We both had issues with alcohol and drugs.

I tackled my issues young. Kevin tried but eventually lost his battle.

We both suffered from severe anxiety and chronic migraines.

My battle continues. Kevin's is over.

We both loved music. We had some different tastes but saw some great concerts together like The Who playing *Quadrophenia* live for the first time.

We loved to do crazy things once in a while like walk through the woods at 1:00 a.m. with headlamps on and see who would be more scared—the people we met, the animals, or us.

We both loved animals. He loved them all. I was only comfortable around dogs when I was with him.

We both loved going for walks in the woods near our house. It was peaceful, and Kevin would stop and say hello to every dog that came by. Sometimes he'd even speak to the humans who were with the dogs.

Kevin and I loved to razz each other. I was "The Putz" to Kevin, and I took joy in razzing him when that perfect moment occurred that every parent waits years for and then—zing!

We differed in some ways: I was a lot bigger than Kevin until he reached the age of thirteen, and then I obviously shrank a lot and he grew a lot.

Kevin always liked to wear black. I wore colours that embarrassed him at times.

I drove; Kevin didn't. And on more than one occasion he mentioned that he didn't think what I was doing should be considered driving either.

Kevin was polite to everyone he met; I'd rather not say any more about that in my defense.

Kevin's addiction started at age fourteen—not even out of high school. At the time, there were no drug programs available for anyone under eighteen, and anxiety programs for youth didn't exist. He did go into recovery programs four different times, and took various anxiety meds and tried behavioural therapies over the next sixteen years. None seemed to help him.

I'm not making excuses for Kevin. He had a pretty stacked deck with addiction, anxiety, and migraines all working against him but he ultimately made his own choices in life.

*I don't want Kevin's life to be defined by his final act of an accidental overdose though.*

Kevin was much more than just an addict. He was a son, a brother, a grandson, a nephew, a cousin, a friend, a godfather, a co-worker, and much, much more to a lot of people who will miss him for the rest of their lives.

All those who knew Kevin are going to miss his infectious laugh and big bear hugs.

Goodbye my big lovable bear.

# 11.
# Sorrow Seasons

TARA MCGUIRE

### SUMMER—GO AWAY

i don't want to talk to you
it hurts
too much
makes all of this real
but oh, it must be
or you wouldn't be here
at my door
with flowers
that look in your eyes
mournful and scared
awkward, yet brave in your arrival
you wouldn't wear that expression

all the twisting feelings you can't possibly articulate
right now
maybe ever
are there in your quivering chin
pressed lips
eyes spilling crimson edged

you don't know what to say
but you try
bless you
you try

with cards and letters
nourishment
feeding the troops who arrive embattled
grappling offers of 'anything i can do'

you try
to poke holes in thick blackness
cultivate a glimmer of light
calls not answered
messages not returned
you try
with love
to plaster the cracks invisible
bless you
thank you

there is nothing else to do
when the only thing i really want

is impossible.

## FALL—MOURNING SICKNESS

Three months have gone by since it happened—it being the sudden death of my son Holden, my beautiful firstborn child.

It wasn't the moment his gorgeous soul left his young body that changed my life. At that moment, I was unaware. It was the moment the tormented police officer walked up our driveway and knocked on our door. Boots heavy, eyes downcast, chin pinched to his broad chest as if bracing for a coming storm, he didn't want to tell me; duty forced his hand. It was a sunny, mild summer afternoon. Why spoil it? "Are you Tara McGuire?" he asked. My young daughter bounced up behind me in our entrance hall to see if one of her friends had dropped by. "Yes" I answered, not knowing this was to be the last moment of peace I would experience for a very, very long time. Our dog crowded the doorway too. She barked deeply at his uniform, his countenance. She didn't want him here. He was dangerous.

"Please come outside. I'd like to talk to you without your daughter." I had no idea why he might know my name and want to speak with me alone. It happened so quickly and unexpectedly that not even a slight shadow of fear crossed my thoughts. Maybe there had been a break-in nearby and he was just going to tell me to make sure and secure the windows at night. I was barefoot and carefree. I had no time to tap the brakes, to prevent him from going any further.

The not knowing was so much better. The quiet just before he spoke expanded and snapped back. It's the out-loudness that makes it true.

My husband, young daughter, and I had recently returned home from a ten-month travelling adventure. After nearly twenty years working for a large broadcasting company my number eventually came up, and like so many other veteran broadcasters, I was fired. I received zero notice and a fat severance package to cushion the blow. Did we decide, like a responsible family living in very expensive Vancouver, to plunk that money on the mortgage? Why of course not. Life is short. Let's make some lemonade. We left for a swirl of international beauty, adventure, and learning. My young adult son Holden would stay home in Vancouver with his father to work and begin building his own independent life. As young adults do. He was twenty-one after all.

On that calm, shorts-and-t-shirt summer day, we were just beginning to get our feet back under us. There was no rush. We were slowly reintegrating with the neighbourhood and discovering what it felt like to be stationary for a change. Our daughter could hop on her bike and set off alone to cruise the neighbourhood. What a novelty. After almost a year of travelling with her parents for constant company, being alone was some kind of thrill.

I distinctly remember exhaling that day, with the simple contentedness of *home*. Home where we know people. Where people know us. Where we can easily read the road signs and the labels at the grocery store. Home where we won't be lost all the time. Home where I can cultivate a new career. Home where we can finally unpack bags that had been stuffed and stinking for nearly a year. Home to family. Holden, who I have missed and worried about the entire time we travelled, is here. He's coming over for dinner tonight after work! The idea of being able to reach over and touch his face while we talk makes me feel like a teenager before a date. I'm so lucky. We are home. Where it's safe.

I remember being aware of how quietly joyful I felt to be unloading groceries and library books from the car. Library books and a jumbo pack of toilet paper meant we were staying. I had a phone number! I could cook for everyone tonight and serve the meal on matching dishes. I was happy.

Standing in the middle of the driveway, under the big leafy Spanish chestnut tree, the police officer got right to it. "Is William Holden Courage your son?" In that instant, looking in his reluctant eyes, I knew he brought the worst possible news. When those words hit my heart ... the world, the universe as I knew it, shattered. And me with it. Or at least, my idea of me. The me who once was, vanished.

The ground fell away, and I was tumbling through space. I could see myself lying curled on the driveway gasping for air. Anyone passing by would have thought I had been shot at close range. The officer tried to fill the spaces between my wailing. I heard words, but they fell on me like snowflakes, quickly melting.

"I'm so sorry ... No sign of foul play ... Don't have that information ... The coroner will investigate. I'm very sorry ... No sign of criminal activity ... He was with a friend ... She's ok. Do you want the trauma team? ... Grief counsellors? ... I'll stay as long as you need me to ... Can we reach your husband? ... How long will it take him to get here? ... Who would you like to call? ... No, it's not a mistake. In the morgue ... I'm so sorry ... Yes, I'm sure ... Yes, it's true ... Yes, he's gone ... Yes ..."

Although many people made assumptions about what had happened that night, we didn't know the facts until many weeks later. Months actually. Holden died of an accidental alcohol and drug overdose. The word "accidental" is an important one to me. We all have accidents. Some of us are here because of an accident. One brief "ah, fuck it" moment. My son didn't mean for this to happen. He had set his alarm for work and gone to sleep. He was just being young and stupid and reckless. I have been all of those things, so I cannot judge. The coroner told me that the amount of drugs alone in his system would likely not have killed Holden. It was the combination of alcohol and drugs together that slowed and eventually stopped his breathing and his astonishing heart.

One of the greatest paradoxes in this story is that that while I revelled in the most beautiful, adventurous, carefree period of my life, Holden was enduring his darkest, most confusing and dangerous phase. Apparently, during the winter we travelled the Indian Ocean, he began experimenting with heavier drugs, as a form of self-medication for his depression and anxiety. He was already a serious drinker and pot smoker, which scared me.

Holden's depression had been a cyclical nemesis for years. I sensed he was in a dark place, as he had been at times before, and asked him about it many times suggesting treatment, books, meditation, rehab. From fifteen thousand kilometres away, he deflected those suggestions and assured me things were okay. "There's nothing to tell you mom. I'm alright." He was often unavailable; the Wi-Fi was iffy, and the time change made it tough to connect.

Why didn't I press him? How could I not have sensed how serious things were getting? We emailed. We skyped. Where was my mother's instinct and protection when he needed them most? Why couldn't I have prevented this? Aside from the black vacuum of his absence, living with these questions and their hollow answers is the hardest part to endure. Why couldn't I protect my child from harm?

When we arrived home I was very relieved to see Holden face to face—to touch him, talk with him, and look him in the eye. We only saw each other once but he appeared healthy. Really great, in fact. His physical presence was reassuring; he would be okay. We spent the evening together talking: he stayed overnight and for breakfast the next morning. His cheeks were rosy after working all day in the hot sun. I told him he seemed robust. "Why thank you; I've been hearing that a lot lately Mutha." He joked in his deep, slow baritone with an amusing hint of an English accent. I thought the dark clouds had passed for good. He was working hard as a landscaper and seemed strong and peaceful. I didn't look deeply enough into those swampy green eyes. I should have asked more questions. I should have listened more carefully. This haunts me.

It must be fall now because the sky is offensively blue, and the leaves are beginning to toast. I sense a slight and uneasy firming of the ground under my feet—a tenuous fraction of a toe hold. The fact that I actually noticed the sky and the trees is a huge discovery. Was it there all along?

Three months have passed in swirling, dense gloom. It has been difficult to see where I am going or find any recognizable reference points to orient myself. Like skiing fast in thick fog, the drops and shocking bumps have been devastating. The sensation of groundlessness and disconnectedness is paralyzing. The first days and weeks I lurched and cartwheeled through space. I curled into a ball. Time lost its natural sequence. My only task—because of the deep love and patience of my husband, daughter, close family, and dear friends—has become simply surviving each day. A strange sort of autopilot has taken over and operates my body while my mind wanders aimlessly down the uncharted paths of why? My occupation is simply waking, walking, crying, sleeping, weeping, and breathing. I try to do normal things that normal people do when this experience is anything but normal.

The first trimester is utter brutality. Just as confirming you will become a mother for the first time is a total shift in your definition of self, so is the beginning of life without that child. Your mind has to work really hard, around the clock, to reorganize the very core of you. You are forever altered, and your psyche has some catching up to do.

Imagine waking up one day to find a new room in your house that never existed before. You keep walking in there confused because this room was not on the original blueprint. Yet there you stand. You keep blinking to be sure it's not a mirage. There are walls to run your hands over and rough wooden floorboards under your feet. There is a window with lace curtains. It is real, it is solid, and it is not going anywhere. Everything you thought to be true, isn't.

Although creating a child can be one of the most beautiful experiences of life and losing one can certainly be the ugliest, there are striking similarities in the physical sensations related to both. I feel sick. All of the time. The nausea of mourning sickness feels the same as maternity morning sickness. Only, crackers don't help, and there's no sweet smelling baby to look forward to when it's over. I am so tired. Unfathomably exhausted. A heavy carpet is draped over me. I cannot lift my head or arms. I have no desire to. I have no appetite, and the smell of certain foods makes me wretch. I sleep like a stupefied zombie: a dreamless log lying in a petrified forest. This must be my body's way of creating a merciful escape—from the truth.

That's where the similarities end.

There is never happiness. If I happen to feel mistakenly cheered, just for a second, guilt instantly rushes in. The vast crater where my heart used to be is now filled with cement. If I fell into the ocean, I would surely be dragged to the bottom by its weight. The choking squeeze in my chest never, ever, goes away. Unlike when I was joyfully pregnant and couldn't wait to begin this new evolution of self as a mother, I would now do anything to peel off this toxic skin. Make it all be untrue, a mistake. One tap from a tiny hammer, and I will disintegrate into dust and be blown away. I wouldn't even mind.

In the early days, it's tough to speak, or God forbid smile, or look anyone in the eye. Eye contact is far too intimate. Food tastes like dirt. Thirst is unquenchable. Taking photos, once a joy, feels offensive. Who would want anyone to document this? Music is too much. The act of lifting my face or unhunching my shoulders for a moment seems too vulnerable. My memory and reflexes are shot. When my rock of a husband brought a stunning bouquet of flowers to me in bed one day, I asked who they were from? "Me," he said, his red eyes welling up. "Happy Anniversary." I had no idea of the date.

I sense a warmth outside where the world continues its spinning, but I am always, always cold. Through this long, hot summer, I have been chilled to the bone. Everything orients down, toward the earth, the frozen centre, the bottom. It's difficult to stand. It is much easier to crawl under the blankets and disappear. This sadness has a pull stronger than gravity, and the only place I can comfortably spend any length of time is in our bed. It cradles my skin and bones as my once strong muscles drip and droop. This bed holds me while my physical body dissolves. All that is left is a notion of who I used to be—a thought, a sigh.

From bed, I can look out and see our big Spanish chestnut tree and watch the shifting shades of green as the leaves dance. Holden loved colour. He was a talented artist. The light subtly shifts as the day changes from bright and sharp to fuzzy pink and blurred. I lie for hours … days … weeks.

From what I recall of morning sickness during pregnancy, the nausea swoops in early in the day. I remember running from the radio studio one morning during Whitney Houston's "I Will Always Love You" to vomit in the staff bathroom. By contrast, mourning sickness, or the phases of processing an enormous loss, comes rampaging in full throttle like bombers on a midnight raid. No warning, no reason, no order. Those chronological stages of grief are bullshit, by the way: denial, isolation, anger, bargaining, depression, and finally acceptance. They don't stand in line and wait their turn to slap you around. They gang up on you. They are a conniving team who use chesslike tactics and strategic manoeuvres to crush you into oblivion. They want every last shred of your joy and will not stop until their insidious mission is accomplished.

There have been infinite hours of deep despair—what if?, and why didn't I?, and if only (bargaining)—and never coming up with one single answer that makes any sense. These questions are unanswerable, which keeps me stirring and roaring round and round (anger) this desolate cave. I don't want anyone in here with me. I want (isolation) to rant alone. Somewhere, deep in the thrashing, a tinkling awareness surfaces that there is no possible way to finesse the outcome in my favour (acceptance). He is gone.

This work is a solo job. Much like giving birth. Yes, there is hand holding, back rubbing, and sincere attempts at comforting. But I alone must push and strain and breathe through the contracting and expanding—the delivering of this new self.

In some ways, I also died that day. The person who was an energetic mother of two is now the fragile mother of one. Where I was once confident and articulate, I am now scared, fumbling, and uncertain. This is the new me.

From the vantage point of three months, I have come to a sort of temporary realization. This place in time feels like a weigh station—a level patch to pull over and check provisions before continuing with the long and arduous journey. More and more, I perceive grief as a physical place. It is a vast, bleak, and horrible wasteland full of traps and dead ends. There are also psychological mirages. There are those moments when the crush lets up for an instant, and I wonder, am I better now? Is the agony over? Will I actually be able to live rather than just exist? Then, in the next moment, the pain gushes back like the tide. Nope, I'm not. It's not. You're not.

This despicable no-man's land is a bleak transition point between the woman I used to be and the one I am to become. I don't want to, but I have no choice. The shifting ground insists on being traversed. These are the badlands between the territory of who I was that warm sunny day before the tall man with the big boots knocked on my door and the foreign soil I must plant my flag on. I am a refugee citizen of a country I was forced to leave. I have been dumped in a strange new land I do not wish to inhabit.

So rather than hurrying to stake my claim and start over in a place where I don't speak the language or understand the customs, I choose to stay a little longer in this desolate zone. I will ruminate a while with my son. I'd rather be here in the bottomless sadness, with him, than there, in a new land, without.

## WINTER—THE HOLE FAMILY

Yesterday marked six months since Holden's exquisite soul left his young body. It was a hard day.

We were tidying up, putting away decorations, tossing wilted poinsettias, and gathering dry boughs and pine cones from the mantle. For some reason, this was even more painful than setting them out had been. The open, clear space created in their absence would normally have meant a fresh feeling of potential for the New Year; instead, it created a powerful vacuum that squeezed my chest with a suffocating longing. I had thought perhaps the vortex was losing some of its pull. I was wrong. The inside of my ribcage rattled like a chandelier in an earthquake. Clattering and swaying.

Some days I feel like I have passed through the worst intensity of the storm and will be able to enjoy life again. The raging has finally begun to subside, and then, like yesterday ... back it all comes. His absence will not be concealed. It is a hole unfillable. I won't even try. I was just sheltered momentarily in the eye of the hurricane.

Wrapping sentimental items in tissue and packing them away in their dark-blue plastic tubs jolted me with its significance. How can we tuck him away so easily? Put him on a shelf until next year? The teddy bear stocking with his name in purple glitter glue, the adorable tree ornaments he made all through school, so achingly sweet. I can picture his tiny hands working earnestly to create them. The proud miniature Christmas tree made of jigsaw puzzle pieces and way too much glue. "Holden—grade one, 1999" in pencil on the back in his careful printing. My favourite, the silver clothes peg angel with her crinkled wings. Then the hardest part, his unopened gifts. Three cans of spray paint, one from each of us. Sky blue, purple, black.

On Christmas Eve, I lit a candle for Holden in his little garden outside under the big tree. That candle stayed lit all night long and well into the next day, enduring the winter wind. Perhaps he wanted us to look to the light? Our pillar of a daughter has been surrounded by her delightful friends, and the sound of their commotion in the house elevated my spirit. I caught myself smiling and laughing in their presence. Such a novel experience I almost wrote down the time and date. Smile: 8:30 p.m., 04/12/15. Laugh: 10:15 a.m., 12/12/15.

People have told me lately that I seem a little bit lighter. I don't see it, but I hope that's true. A gradual melting. It would be so very easy to dwell forever in this place of sadness. I heard of one woman who took to her bed for three years after her son died. Honestly, it is a tempting option that I have seriously considered. But I have to believe there is a reason to walk out of the darkness and back into my life. Whatever that means. And not just for my husband and daughter who I feel deserve it, for me too.

Through these dark days, I have observed a deep thoughtfulness from the outside world—in heartfelt notes, letters and emails, sneaky gifts left on our porch, quiet hugs. I have reflected often and with deepest gratitude on these sincere kindnesses. They have helped me to feel less alone.

The most meaningful and beautiful offering is when others have told me that they don't really know what to do or say but are willing to try anyway. We are all on quicksand here. People have attempted to show me how they care, how they love and remember Holden, and how they will continue to be there for us. They have shared losses and fears openly and honestly. They have asked fumbling questions. Our collective humanness has been revealed.

I don't know what this new year will bring or what it means for our family. There never was any certainty; I'm just more aware of that fact now. I suppose I am becoming more comfortable being lopsided. Where there used to be four toothbrushes now there are three. We are a three-legged table. Still a table, but wobbly. As some wise people who have walked this road before me have advised, I'm learning to wade into the pain. Fully experiencing and processing it whenever it happens to arrive. Like it did today.

When I see his graffiti around the city, it shakes me. When I smell something earthy and grassy like his t-shirts in my bottom drawer or his sheets in the linen closet it surfaces. When I see a young man walking down the road with his pants hung low and his big shoes flapping like flippers at ten and two o'clock, the crush surges directly to my heart, and I feel it all again. Six months have passed, and I have learned to let it rise—to let the pain wash and surge through me when and how it decides. It seems like the only way.

There is a hole in me, in our family, a big one. We are a hole family now.

### SPRING—WITHOUT

on Sunday

i will wake disappointed
again as so many times before to find it's true
from the other side now the back of motherhood
hoodmother

corners dusty circle closed

on Sunday i will cherish you
it was you who made me a mother

close my eyes to kiss fat toes
scoop round belly
run silken hair through fingers

oh the smell the smell of my own child.
well before you were born you were mine and so
well after you are gone you are still

and always.

on Sunday i will spread my blanket for all mothers
whose mom-ness didn't go as planned
for her for you i will breathe deep exhale gaze to blue and pray
she who longed and wished and waited pleading
please please unanswered prayers
she who suffered miscarried the stillborn the aborted the never
quite made it
hopeful embers who refused to ignite
she who raised those born of others and loved them close
i remember you i know you yes we have met.

on Sunday you are a mother all and truly
you birthed the glow of love
you delivered a promise unkeepable
you nurtured a craving unmet never forgotten

on Sunday for the ones who
eat no pancakes place no flowers in a jar answer no echoing long
distance phone calls
i honour you with reverence.

i see you now and
i am sorry to not have noticed you standing there before enduring
Sundays past

for all the sparks that rose from the fire too soon
blinking off into the night ahead of schedule

on Sunday please recall the bedrock truth
you were part of a miracle once and
a miracle that doesn't last
is still a miracle

# 12.
# Worlds Apart

## BECKY LIVINGSTON

UNLESS YOU'D HAVE LOOKED CLOSELY, you wouldn't have noticed the scar. Her natural waves camouflaged it well. Shaped like the letter C, it scored a line that severed her scalp, tucked neatly behind her left ear where the skin was still a little pink. Inflamed.

There were no tears at the airport, only nervous laughter and mild restraint. Hugs were big and firm; kisses quick. "Safe travels." "Love you." "Have fun." Five months in New Zealand. Alone.

"Phone me once a week."

At eighteen, and with the all-clear from the doctors, she was off. Some questioned our decision, her condition so raw. Bob, my fiancé, his arm around my waist, pulled me in tight to his side, kissed my head.

"She'll be fine."

My daughter, Rachel, bristling with promise. A young woman who'd mastered young the art of living with uncertainty. With questions that have no answers. The big one: How long would radiation keep the brain tumour from returning. A year? Two years? Ten?

For Rachel, it was five. She was twenty-three years old.

It's not the first time I've acted against my better judgment. This time it descended upon me some thirteen months after Rachel died, in what I think now was the very worst of my grief. Nothing was as bad for me as early on in the second year. Those were the days when I had no idea how to carry on living. Absolutely none.

That's when I went hiking in the woods.

People warn the recently bereaved: "Don't do anything foolish. Something you might regret." In the clutches of grief, conventional wisdom tells us to keep going. Eat well. Get outside every day. Sleep as much as you need. Set a daily goal. Be gentle with yourself but don't get soft. Reach out when you're ready. And be careful with addictive substances. But red wine and rage, I'd discovered long ago, make a perfect pairing.

Something had to change. Walking in nature often shifted my mood. Sabotaging good judgment, I took a route I'd never hiked before: Eagleridge Bluffs. An old growth forest. Douglas firs. Cedars. Deep roots. Wide branches. Two hours trekking, and I was lost. Three hours. Still lost. No path was clear. There were no tracks in the snow.

In February, the light fades quickly, a hazard that catches many hikers off guard. On Vancouver's North Shore Mountains it happens all the time. I imagine a search and rescue team out searching for me. Me? Now there would be a story. My despair fully exposed.

Peter had bailed. I hadn't realized. Not for months.

"I'm glad you were with me till the end."

"I wasn't," he said.

We never talked about what that really meant. But I made a point of remembering it. Because the truth is, neither of us could handle my grief. The more I closed in the further he ran. (Try talking with the man you love about anything other than your daughter dying.) I never asked, "Will you stay with me through all this?" I was terrified that he might not.

Higher and higher I climbed, as if some kind of answer was waiting there at the top. Closer to the sky. A clearing?

*Nobody would miss me.* Not until my absence at school tomorrow morning. I relished the thought. Last week, a teacher's comment had flung me into a rage. She'd touched me on the shoulder. "She's always with you," her voice, so pious. That tone, of all the things people said, made this the worst.

Then it happened. Lost in thought one moment, the next, I was hovering over a dizzying height—my hiking boot inches from going over.

I looked down. Below me, the ground fell away. The bottom, I could just make out. The drop off was well below what a body could withstand were it to fall.

Just one more step.

All this time looking down, I'd lost focus.

Rachel was gone. Bob was gone. Peter too. Where was home without them? So this is how despair feels: a death wish and life wish both desperate for victory. I can't tell which side of the life-death continuum I'm on.

But there's Charlotte. My living daughter.

There's me.

My heart thumps. Alive.

Ankles locked. Swaying. Left. Right. Left. There it was. The end of Howe Sound. A landmark. I was heading in the completely wrong direction.

Down there somewhere, my luxurious oversized sofa, where in the deep down-filled cushions, I'd realized the great tragedy. "Accepting" my loss meant I was getting better. But getting better, or healing, or admitting the truth, whatever you want to call it, could only happen if I reconciled myself to the truth—I'd have to live life without her. How could I give myself this permission? I didn't want to stop grieving. I couldn't. Grieving kept her close. To get on with life felt like abandoning her.

I could feel the tears rising up in me. Then come. Hot. Stinging. The wind dried them to my cheek, a tight white.

As I lurched back from the edge, a giant branch snagged my leg, lodging into the flesh of my calf through my thick hiking pants. No one heard me cry. I slid my hand inside my pants, shocked by my body's response to fear—a warm wetness between my legs.

Then I decided to do something I'd never done before or thought I ever would. I hugged a tree. A giant Douglas fir. Glad then, that nobody could see me.

Is this what it has come to?

I'd read about those people further up the coast who did this kind of thing to save the forests. Tree-huggers. A photograph of a woman with her palms pressed against the trunk of a giant cedar, her head lowered between her outstretched arms, had consumed an entire page of the magazine. I was not one of these earthy women. I didn't want to be. But some lines from a poem, I suddenly remembered now:

Stand still. The forest knows
Where you are. You must let it find you
If what a tree or a bush does is lost on you,
You are surely lost.
—David Wagoner, "Lost"

My hot cheek against the scruffy bark, I called a truce. It was oddly silent, as if the world was through with me, heard me holding on. I brushed my fingertips along the coarse, slimy grooves and whispered into the woody mustiness of a damp tree.

"I'm sorry."

What happened after that I don't recall only that I needed to find the helipad. Take refuge in an open sky.

"They built it for the new four-lane highway for the Olympics," a hiker told me some weeks back.

A memory. Unbidden. The Olympic Torch Relay. My ex-husband, Rachel's father, had carried her in a bear paw pouch around his neck. Her ashes were only a week old.

Helipads, I realized only then, are placed in the highest locations. That quick exit to the sky.

All have a path leading away.

A mother remembers what she must do. To revive her skewered heart, she must keep going. That will be her refuge. Risk life for just one more day. If Rachel's death led me to this cliff-edge moment, it also made me find my way without her.

I didn't tell anyone what really happened. I just made it a funny story at school the next day.

# 13.
# Christmases

JANE DAVEY-KEOGH

ON THE MORNING OF 20 January 2004, my seventeen-year-old daughter, Emily, got into her car to drive to South Carleton High School in Richmond, Ontario, to write her grade-twelve English exam. She never came back home. She lost control of her car on black ice and hit an oncoming City of Ottawa truck. She died instantly.

I didn't know when I left our house to go to work a bit later that morning my life would never be the same again. In my car, I turned on the radio, and as I did, the announcer reported there had been a serious car accident on a rural stretch of road near our home. I listened carefully. I heard the driver of the car, a woman, was seriously injured. I felt relieved when I heard that. I told myself it couldn't be my daughter; she was seventeen, a teenager, not yet a woman. Yet somehow I knew that I might be fooling myself. I started to shake and held the steering wheel tight. Panic set in. I turned my car around to drive to the scene of the accident, but the road was barricaded off. I ran out of my car and raced to get past the barricade. I had to know. I had to see if it was Emily's car. A police officer noticed me and held me back. When I told him my name, he took me to his police cruiser and left me in the backseat for what seemed like eternity. Alone. Frantic, unable to get out of the car. Then I heard this on the police radio: "Next of kin is in the cruiser." I knew.

My world turned upside down, and I didn't know how to turn it right side up.

Emily was smart, popular, beautiful, and wise—an honour student, rugby team co-captain, and a student council member. I was the luckiest mother. She was my daughter and my friend. Now she was dead. I felt like I was watching someone else, not me. I didn't know how to understand what had happened or how to grapple with what was so unreal, so sudden.

That afternoon, back at home, I worried about how to tell her brother who was away at university that she was dead. Emily's friends phoned: "What happened? Is Emily okay? She didn't come to school for the exam." I didn't cry—I couldn't—not that day and not at her funeral.

For a long time, I walked around in a daze. I was numb, stunned. My brain knew Emily died, but my heart did not. My heart could not fathom the fact that this was not a dream, that I would never see my child again, and that I would never watch her fall in love or become a parent. I couldn't understand how I was supposed to live the rest of my days without my child. My future was ruined; I didn't even have a future any more. Nothing in life was worthwhile, nothing mattered. I felt hopeless and I finally understood the saying "she died of a broken heart."

My heart was raw and filled with anger, frustration, betrayal, and sadness. Sadness was the biggest emotion for me to deal with. I did not know human beings could feel such deep, deep painful sorrow. Any sadness I had felt before my child died was a drop in the bucket compared to the sadness I felt now. A dark cloud hung over my head, and I couldn't escape it. There was no light at the end of the tunnel for me. I was diagnosed with clinical depression.

I could not return to work for thirteen months, and I was lucky that I was enough of a basket case to qualify for long-term disability through my work. For the first nine months, each day was spent the same way. I slept on and off for thirteen hours and woke up at one in the afternoon. I ate breakfast/lunch. I took my dog for a one-hour walk ... because people told me I needed to get exercise and fresh air ... it would make me feel better. Huh! I came home and watched the show *Crossing Over with John Edwards*. He was a medium who connected with the dead and brought messages to their loved ones left here on earth. I needed to believe the spirit lived on because that gave me hope I would see my child again when I died. I scoured the obituaries for other children who had died so I would feel as though I was not the only parent in the world dealing with the death of a child. Sometimes people called me or came to visit me. I cooked dinner for my husband. I ate dinner. I watched television, but I didn't take in the shows because my mind wandered to my grief. I went to bed for thirteen hours. Repeat.

I didn't know how to fix myself. And I needed to because living like this was unbearable. I needed to know when I was going to feel better, when I would feel the dark cloud lift, when there would be a sense of hopefulness instead of hopelessness. Diagnosed with clinical depression, I decided to start trying to fix myself. I saw a grief counsellor. She came to my house, and we talked. She became my one-hundred-dollar-an-hour friend. For that hour, I felt better just talking to her. I was doing some things right. I got outside for exercise and fresh air. People came to visit me so I was socializing.

I needed to set aside a specific time each day to think of Emily, cry, and grieve. That way, I would be more in charge of my grief and not let my grief overcome me at inopportune moments—like when the checkout woman at the grocery store says "Hi, how are you?" I read some books on grief and learned that what I was feeling was normal, even though I felt far from normal.

Three friends, Barbara, Jill and Kuo, listened without judgment and let me talk and talk and talk about my daughter and my grief. I joined an eight-week closed support group at Bereaved Families of Ontario for loss of child. For the first time since my child died, I felt normal. I belonged. We were all angry and sad, and we were a great support to each other—more so than my family and friends because they got me. I learned to be grateful and appreciate what I had in life instead of focusing on what I didn't have. I learned that there are people out there even worse off than me. There were parents who had lost two children.

But I still needed to know how long I would feel horrible. Nobody seemed to be able to answer that question. It took five years before I felt like I was going to make it. The progress was so slow that I didn't even notice any progress until years had passed, and I could look back on my grief journey. I wore mascara again for the first time on the eighth anniversary of my daughter's death. Progress.

Thirteen years later, I can say that I have found peace with my loss. I am happy. My focus, memory, and concentration have returned. I cherish my relationships. My energy has returned, and I can reinvest it in things I enjoy.

I am now a volunteer facilitator at Bereaved Families of Ontario. I help other bereaved parents who have lost a child. I feel no parent should have to endure the task of grieving a child alone. I am just a regular parent who could not carry on with her daily living, and I made it through the worst of the grief process and came out the other end. I have the energy to help others. Some people question why I would want to continually go back and revisit my grief. Isn't there something more cheery I could do, instead? But I feel privileged to do this and honoured that parents are willing to be vulnerable and share their intense grief with me. Other than raising two children, this is the most rewarding thing I've ever done.

## MY FIRST CHRISTMAS WITHOUT EMILY

Holidays throughout the first year were difficult. I made it through family birthdays, Mother's Day, Easter, and Emily's birthday. They were difficult because I thought of her more those days than I usually did—and I thought of her a lot. In fact, most of my waking moments were consumed by her and her death. I had no idea, however, how to make it through Christmas.

Lucky for me (as if losing a child and lucky should ever be used in conjunction with each other), she died in January, and I had eleven months before I would have to spend my first Christmas without her. I started thinking about my Christmas in September. Christmas season lasts so very long, as decorations and music in stores start the morning after Halloween. People start asking you what you are doing for Christmas. They tell you to "have a nice Christmas" and "I hope you have a great time with all of your family." They don't understand how painful that is. How can I possibly spend Christmas with all of my family when all of them are not here? Some people told me how I should spend Christmas without her. Their advice made me angry, but I realized they were trying to help; they just didn't know how. And I am thankful they didn't know because the only way they would know is if they too had lost a child. And I wouldn't wish that fate on anyone.

I didn't know how to go shopping for others, as I would see gifts my daughter would love but could not buy for her. I didn't know how to go to stores and see other moms shopping with their teenage daughter. How could I walk by the Laura Secord ice cream and not be reminded that it was always our last mother and daughter shopping stop before going home?

And I didn't know how I was going to decorate a tree. I bought her an ornament every year reflecting something going on in her life that year—a bear kicking a soccer ball, a rolling pin for baking pies, a suitcase for her trip to Florida. It was too painful to take all those ornaments out of the box and look at them. I didn't know how I was going to figure out the stocking thing either.

Do I pull out everyone's stocking but leave hers in a box in the basement? Do I put hers out with the rest of ours but see hers empty on Christmas morning when everyone else's is full? It wrenched my heart whenever I thought about my son having to go downstairs and peek at his stocking without his sister. They always woke each other up and went downstairs to look at their stocking together before coming back upstairs to wake me up. They did this even when they were sixteen and eighteen.

I felt a strong need to buy her something or do something for her. How could I do that when she is no longer here? Then, through my pain, I remembered previous Christmases when Emily and her brother would help me make and decorate gingerbread houses, a tradition of ours. I decided to make gingerbread houses and sell them. A scholarship fund had been set up in her memory at her high school, and I would donate the proceeds of the houses. This would allow me to do something for her, but in her memory. The most gingerbread houses I'd ever made at one time was four, so in my fuzzy grief brain, it only seemed reasonable that I should make and sell fifty. Making the gingerbread houses helped me to get through the Christmas season. I didn't put up any ornaments or a tree that year, and our stockings were plastic grocery bags.

Christmas Day was difficult. It was so obvious and sad that Emily was missing. I cried before I even got out of bed that morning. The dreaded day was here. We went downstairs and opened our grocery bags. We all tried to put on brave faces for each other, but we all knew inside we were hating this day. After opening the stockings, we ate breakfast. I cried while preparing it because

Emily and I always prepared it together, and now I was preparing it alone in the kitchen. As we ate in silence, my son became teary eyed. I, too, cried yet again.

At noon, my son left to go to his dad's place, alone, and without his sister. I cried again because it was so sad that he couldn't share Christmas with her. I felt so bad for my son, but I was happy he was gone because I couldn't feel his sadness any more. And it allowed me to escape to my bedroom and cry and sleep for the rest of the afternoon. Being able to sleep away the afternoon was the best part of my Christmas Day.

I declined invitations to dinners with family and friends. I couldn't bear to spend Christmas dinner with other people's families when part of my family was missing. Watching other families being happy together when I was so unhappy was a cruel punishment for me to inflict on myself. I went to bed on Christmas night, and I felt a huge weight lifted off my shoulders and a huge sense of accomplishment that I made it through my first Christmas.

I still wish Christmas Day didn't exist. I still have never hung up any ornaments, and the stockings remain in a box in the basement. I have put up one tree in thirteen years. It is still so sad for me that my son doesn't get to spend Christmas with his sister. I still make gingerbread houses every year. Making these houses is my Christmas. Friends and family still come over to help, and the project has become a tradition for many people in my life; it eases my pain of Christmases without her. When we are busy making the gingerbread houses, my home is filled with people. We do this in her memory.

And it has grown. My extended family has a North Vancouver branch operation that makes fifty houses a year. I make two hundred houses a year. My living room, dining room, and kitchen become the manufacturing facility for six weeks of the year. People who buy a gingerbread house tell me they think of Emily when they bring their gingerbread to their home. As a parent who has lost a child, I feel good knowing my child is remembered by others. Because as a parent, I will never forget.

Early on, someone told me that time heals. It made me angry because time was not healing me. Looking back, I can say that a combination of working through grief in conjunction with time did help. I now feel hope. I can laugh and have a good time. I still don't understand why my child died, but I accept that she did.

I have come out of a very dark place where I was for a very long time.

My Christmases have never been the same since Emily died, and I know they never will be. But I am glad I have found my way to do something for my loved one in her memory at Christmas.

# 14.
# Memory Box

JUDY LYNNE

THE MEMORY BOX RESTS in the hall below the wooden book-shelves. Coated in a lustrous red and black lacquer and embossed with a floral folk art design, it is the perfect vessel for the precious remains now resting within its sturdy walls. Among the treasures nestled inside are my son's journal, his Christmas stocking, a Marge Simpson Pez dispenser, his Whistler ski patrol fleece, an avalanche transceiver, a photograph album, and a Boursin cheese box. This small trunk now cradles a selection of keepsakes from a young life fully lived.

On a Saturday night in mid-April, Vancouver was wet and unseasonably warm, and I had been dancing the Shim Sham Shimmy with five other women—performing for an audience of mostly friends. My daughter, Lucy, a dancer and the baby of the family, had taught us the choreography the previous week. Adorned in a stringy, glittering black chemise, long pearls, a velvet headband, and ostrich plume affixed to one side with a rhinestone pin, I was having fun.

There were messages on my phone when I arrived home around midnight. Four of them. All from Scott, my eldest child. All telling me to call him as soon as I got home. The third message convinced me it couldn't wait until morning. I could hear Sandra, his girlfriend, in the background. And then, Scott again: "it doesn't matter how late it is; you must phone me." And so I did.

He had bad news. I could hear Sandra. Something about "not on the phone," and so he asked me, "Do you want me to come over?"

My head began to feel light, empty. "Just tell me what it is."

"Neil is dead." I felt nothing but icy cold. Scott was saying he would be over in fifteen minutes.

When he arrived, he told me the RCMP had come to his flat at 8:00 p.m. They said his brother "had passed." He didn't understand. And then he did. And then he had to be strong. He had to tell his mother that Neil had fallen into the Wapta Icefield below Balfour High Col in the Alberta Rockies.

I hadn't known about the trip. My middle child had learned not to tell me about his exploits until they were over; it was better to relay the highlights of his adventures once he had completed them so that Mum didn't worry.

Lucy, the baby of the family, was in Portland, Oregon, at a Swing Dance Festival. When I reached her by phone at 1:00 a.m., she dropped to the floor screaming, "No, No, No." I knew she was with caring friends.

Neil had journeyed through the Wapta Icefield Ski Traverse—a wilderness trek heralded as one of the most spectacular in the world—with two Whistler friends: Greg McDonnell and Dave Smith. His journey of a lifetime began with a glorious day of skiing in Golden, British Columbia. The next morning, the weather had shifted. Visibility was intermittent when they entered the Peyto Glacier and conditions remained difficult for the next three days. On the third night, they met two other skiers—Sean Fraser from Prince George and Eric de Nys of Calgary—and took shelter in the Balfour Hut, twenty-eight kilometres northwest of Lake Louise. The five men decided to join forces in the morning; they skied roped together to the base of Balfour Peak and planned to take shelter at another hut on the northwest shoulder of Mount Daly, expecting to ski out into Lake Louise, a tourist village in Banff National Park, on the fifth day of their traverse.

When they reached the Balfour High Col below Balfour Peak, they were in extreme whiteout. The flat blanket of sky was indistinguishable from the snow beneath them. They decided to unrope and move as a unit, almost touching, because of the limited visibility so that they could communicate with one another. Greg saw Neil move to the left, take three pole plants, and then silently disappear.

That was when they realized they were off route and right on the edge of the Col, several hundred feet above the icefield. Calling to Neil elicited no response. Getting safely to him in the whiteout meant following the ridge northeast down to an area where one of them could ski across to where Neil had toppled. The risk of setting off an avalanche meant sending only one of them, preferably the lightest. Sean, a forest firefighter, was the smallest and had the most medical training.

When Sean found Neil, about eighty minutes after his fall, he was face down in the snow. He had no pulse. My beautiful, strong, and vibrant son was dead. It was the morning of Friday 12 April 2002. News of his death would not reach me for another thirty-five hours.

Months later, at Christmas, I asked Greg what Neil's last words had been. "I'll never forget," he replied. It was just after the group had unroped, reassembled, and arranged to move together. Neil plopped his goggles back on and in the vernacular of his favourite cartoon character, Homer Simpson, he said "Doh! Who turned off da lights?" Minutes later, he vanished.

Lucy arrived back in Vancouver around midnight on Sunday night. She and Scott crept up to my bedroom and crawled under the covers with me, waking me from an Ativan-induced sleep with the most tender of embraces.

My three children had always been close despite family turmoil, divorce, and an ugly custody battle. They learned to create meaning and to make sense of their peculiar, confusing family. They were, in a way, each other's best friends.

The support of my own friends carried me through those awful first days. I had discovered feminism in the early 1970s, and by 1976, I had come out as a lesbian inspired by the strength, courage, and love of so many women before me. Neil's death evoked a deep appreciation of my caring community. From the moment I was able to speak this painful tragedy, my women friends rearranged their lives, their work, and their children and families. We were fed, consoled, held, and rocked. They gently consulted with me, assisted with arrangements for the treatment of Neil's body in Calgary, and booked our flights to see him once his body was evacuated from the mountain.

Friends planned and arranged for Neil's Vancouver memorial—always with deference to me and my children. That sometimes meant quietly reminding my children they may need to grant me the final word. My intuitions were trusted and validated without question, and I felt unconditionally supported and heard in all of the difficult choices that were made over those agonizing days. My heart, my belly from whence Neil entered the world, my back, and my head were massaged with the most tender, unconditional love, and silence. Some of that care was simply allowing us time and space to absorb what had happened to so suddenly change our lives.

On the Tuesday following Neil's death, in the midst of their own trauma, Greg and Dave came down from Whistler to be with us and fill in details about their beautiful and devastating journey and to help us write a fitting obituary. Chris, Neil's best friend from high school days, and three other Whistlerites came with them to support us and share memories.

I was sitting in the living room with Lucy, Scott, and my friend Kathryn. A fire blazed in the fireplace despite the early afternoon sunshine pouring through the tall windows and skylight of my loft. Since hearing the news of Neil's death, I had not been able to get warm. Shivering under an old quilt my maternal grandmother had made, I exchanged hugs, tears, and gratitude.

Questions about Neil and the journey were gently answered; stories and anecdotes were revealed about his humour, his daring, his generosity, his love of the mountains and powder snow, and all the things they wanted never to forget. Lucy captured it all on paper to distill into a final tribute.

Photos of the ill-fated trek were shared: images of a happy, robust Neil with his buddies, magnificent snowy alps, the reflection of a camera in the right lens of his sunglasses. And then a close-up of a raven in profile. "It's Neil!" I said. "Who took this photograph?"

Greg leaned over my shoulder. "Neil did."

"He's taken a picture of himself." The raven was in profile, looking into the distance. I'd seen Neil in that place, in the mountains or ocean kayaking—lost in the moment, enchanted by his surroundings. This was Neil. A second picture captured the same raven in flight.

"That raven, actually two ravens, followed us throughout the trip. Neil really connected with them. He stood still for half an hour with a piece of chocolate in his hand, waiting for the raven to take it. They are huge birds, two and a half times the size of a crow. Amazing how they survive so far above the tree line, just following crumbs left by humans," Greg said.

Cans of cold beer were cracked open, and a projector and screen were set up to indulge us with more photos. They moved on to planning the memorial that would happen in Whistler in just a few days. Who would they ask to emcee? What music? Film clips of Neil? Refreshments? The mayor of Whistler would of course be there. Accommodations would have to be arranged for all of our family. A helicopter flyover ceremony could be organized and happen simultaneously with all the patrollers, in uniform, skiing down the mountain at dusk wearing headlamps—a fitting tribute to their friend. I tried to imagine all this ceremony and wondered that my middle child could generate such pageantry in death.

And then the tipping point. "We could arrange for images of Neil to be projected on a big screen in Whistler Village near the lift," someone offered.

"Yeah! Great idea! I'll contact...." Their muffled sounds resonated somewhere in the distance. At first, they didn't notice me curled in a fetal position under the staircase, rocking back and forth, and sobbing, "He's just a boy! Don't make him into a hero."

Recalling that day now, I feel a sense of gratitude. I was exhausted. The enthusiasm of his friends and their desire to raise my child up onto a pedestal had dislodged my grief—moving it beyond cold and numb. The scene playing out in my mind was of young people witnessing larger than life photos of my child projected onto the buildings and walls of Whistler Village. What message would it send? Some universal parental responsibility whispered inside my head: I want him remembered, not worshipped.

Kathryn had the grace and wisdom to thank them for their assistance in creating memories that would help us write a tribute for the newspaper. She suggested they gather up the beer, projector, and pictures, and leave us to create the obituary. They understood.

My ex-husband also needed to be considered. Scott had called his father with the news, and Keith had called me from his home in Florida. We had not had a happy marriage. Following our breakup, on the few occasions we were in the same room, I simply went through the motions of being nice. He had called now to give me advice. "I hope you aren't planning to see his body. It won't be pretty. You'll always remember him like that." He had given the same advice to Scott and Lucy.

I couldn't imagine not seeing my son's body. It was still too soon to know if he would ever leave the place where he lay buried, but the RCMP knew his location, and he was wearing a transceiver. If the weather cleared enough for them to fly over the area, they should be able to pick up his signal. I called Greg to ask if Sean had described to them what Neil looked like when he reached him.

"Are you sure you want me to tell you on the phone?"

"Yes. I want to know." I was sitting in a chair at the dining room table, directly under the skylight. Lucy and Scott were on either side of me. He told me, carefully choosing his words.

I heard a sound, a kind of wail that rose up and through the skylight sixteen feet above my head. Lucy and Scott were crouched down, clutching my chair to keep it from falling over and me with it.

I don't remember telling them what Greg had conveyed, or them asking. I remember them holding me. I hadn't given any thought to how my children might be affected by my grief. They had never seen their mother in such torment.

Lucy and Scott went quietly up to my bedroom. When they came back down the stairs, Scott was three or four steps behind Lucy. As they moved into the living room, I was fixed on the space between them. It moved with them—the space that Neil would have filled. He had been the glue that held us together. He had been the bridge when his father and I separated and his big brother went to live with their dad. He assigned himself the role of family fixer, and now all I could see was a humongous empty space.

Lucy took the risk of voicing their concern. The depth of my pain had frightened them both. They said the moan I had made did not sound human. Lucy called it primordial. I didn't know it had come from me.

She struggled over what she needed to say for the two of them. They feared I might not want to go on living.

I had never wanted to live more than I did in that moment. But how would they have known that? They needed to hear that no amount of pain was going to make me abandon keeping Neil's memory alive. That's my job. It's what mothers do.

It was also the confirmation I needed that I would, absolutely, view Neil's body if he were found. I had to know it was him. I needed proof. A week later, just before entering the room at the funeral home in Calgary, I turned to Scott and said, "Maybe it won't be Neil. If it's not him, we will have to start looking for him. We will need to find him." But it was him. My son really was dead.

## FINDING COMFORT AND HEALING

Since the late 1990s, I have been a member of a women's dream group that meets monthly to share dreams and consider what messages they hold for us. When I am able to capture dreams on paper before they escape, the messages they provide can be intensely personal information. Sometimes they come as comfort. When I am open to their gifts, they can be healing. That healing began when the raven came to visit.

It was on the Thursday, a week after Neil's death. One of the Lake Louise RCMP staff had called to say that the forecast indicated clearing skies overnight and early Friday. They were confident a rescue helicopter and crew would be able to fly into the area to search for Neil's body. My hands shook so that the receiver rattled and fell off the cradle. When my breathing steadied, I went up to my bedroom to just be with Neil. Moments after lying down, I felt a distinct tug on my left foot—movement, a light weight along my legs, rippling up my body and lying heavily across my chest. It was comforting, a wingspan from shoulder to shoulder.

The visit was brief, and the weight lifted before I was willing to let it go. Where did the raven in the picture go after Neil fell? Greg and Dave said the raven followed them throughout the trip. I rose and phoned Greg in Whistler. "The ravens—did they follow you out of the mountains? Did you see them after Neil fell? Were they with you when Neil fell?"

"I don't know. Visibility was poor. They may have been behind us. I don't really know. Neil was more connected with them than the rest of us were."

I rang the RCMP in Lake Louise. "Can you get a message to the rescue crew? Can you ask them to observe if there's a raven in the area where Neil's body is?"

The officer was doubtful. "Ravens follow people for food. Conditions have been so bad all week that there are no people up there for them to follow." But he assured me he would pass my message on to the rescue team.

The next morning at 8:30 a.m., the phone rang. It was a female RCMP officer. "Neil's body has just been evacuated. He's on his way to Canmore. From there, he will be taken to the medical examiner's office in Calgary. He was buried under more than a metre of snow," she told me. "And Ms. Lynne," she added, "there was a raven where Neil was found. The helicopter frightened it away coming over the col, but it was there."

There were other dreams. One came in early July, on the day before I would go to Lake Louise and be flown by helicopter above the journey Neil had taken. In the dream, Neil and I are entering a foreign country on foot. There are border guards at the entrance to a village. We are allowed in, and we walk through a busy market to the outskirts of the town and then along a narrow, dusty path. Neil takes out his lunch and sits on one side of the path facing me. I am on the other side. He is smiling as he says to me, "If anyone had told me I would be in the place I am now, I would never have believed them." I woke up feeling comforted.

### THE COMPASSIONATE FRIENDS

A friend had come by in that first week to drop off a book of poetry titled *Holding On: Poems for Alex*. The author, Cathy Sosnowsky, had written a collection of grief poems for her teenage son who died in an accident in 1994. She facilitated a Compassionate Friends chapter in North Vancouver, and I was given her contact information.

The book of poetry was written eight years after the death of Cathy's only birth child. The beginning poems are intense cries from those early years of despair. Others convey a passing of time, changing insights, and tender, whimsical memories.

Lucy saw the book sitting on the dining room table. "Ah! Cathy—you met her! Remember?" I had met Cathy at Langara College when she presented Lucy with an English award. It had been a mere two years after Alex's death, and Lucy recalled me puzzling why Cathy would talk to me, a perfect stranger, about the death of her son. I remembered her telling me how much she had enjoyed having Lucy as a student, and then how the conversation had turned to Alex and his death while doing something mischievous as teenage boys will do. On the way home in the car, I had expressed surprise and curiosity that her professor would have shared such loss and grief with a complete stranger.

Now I am a member of this new tribe of strangers who understand all too well the need to talk about the child who is no longer here. It is a good reminder in those times when I sense discomfort or surprise as I speak of my dead son with someone who, thankfully, doesn't understand.

Reconnecting with Cathy felt somehow precious, to hear about Alex, and to know that this could be me in eight years—recalling Neil, still tearing up with a mixture of sorrow, joy and recaptured memory. Cathy introduced me to The Compassionate Friends—a support group for bereaved parents. I attended one of the monthly gatherings two months into my loss. It became a safe and welcoming home where I sometimes imagined our dead children together as a special kind of family.

Through my relationship with the Compassionate Friends, Lucy and I created a quilt piece to add to the North Shore Compassionate Friends collaborative quilt. It features a photograph of Neil skiing on Whistler Mountain, a single raven overhead.

### OTHER WAYS OF HEALING

My children had their own grieving and healing to do. Scott took care of himself more privately with the support of his love, Sandra, now his wife and the mother of their eight-year-old son. In one of his tributes to Neil, Scott spoke of how hard it was enduring the confusion of his parents' separation, but "I had three things going for me—my bike, my dog Sandy, and my brother." Lucy remained close to me and Scott, but I believe it was alone with her partner, Aaron, that she found the silence and support to embrace her despair.

As a dancer, Lucy had a large community of friends. With her permission, I share an excerpt of a letter she wrote to her dance community on 21 May 2002:

*I know that I may be a difficult person to be around for a while, especially the first few times you see me. You may not know what to say or do, and you may be confused by my behaviour. That's ok.*

*I am covetous of my grief: I want it. I want it to rock me and shake me and rip the ground out from under my feet. I want it to wash through me and soothe me.*

*I know that there is no way around my grief; I must go through it. I am wary of impulses that suggest an inclination to avoid the hard stuff.*

*I appreciate expressions of sympathy, or simple acknowledgment of why I've been away from the scene, but I'm often perplexed as to how to respond because my feelings vary greatly.*

*What can you do?*

*Know that I loved my brother deeply and that I think of him often. Don't worry about reminding me of him. I like to think of him. Besides, no one living has the power to suppress such thoughts and memories. They come and go as they will.*

*Offer expressions of sympathy if you want to, whenever you want to. I know it's often easier to say "be genuine" than to actually follow through, especially if you're feeling awkward, but "be genuine." If you don't know what to say, say that.*

*Ask me about Neil. Ask me about my relationship with him. Be sure, if you do, that the time and setting allow for me to do justice to the question.*

*If I'm more curt than usual, try not to take it personally. My world is, for a while, much smaller, and my reactions are more visceral.*

*Thank you for caring enough to read this and to be someone I feel comfortable sharing it with.*

*Lucy*

I have other family too. Jennie was Neil's high school sweetheart. A no-nonsense teen, Jennie was a strong outdoors woman; a rock climber, kayaker, and camper. She had clear boundaries and spoke her mind. Hiking with Jennie on Mount Seymour brought out the adventurer in Neil. Unfortunately, when his guy friends started needling him about spending too much time with a girl, eighteen-year-old Neil erred on the side of the guys and the relationship took a dive.

Lucy and I had maintained our connection with Jennie who by the time of Neil's death was married and living in Edmonton, Alberta. She and Neil had reconnected by phone a few months before he died when he had called to wish her a happy birthday. They had made plans to get together, go on a hike, share a meal, and have some laughs over their tender past. A reconnection had been made, but their visit never happened.

Instead, Jennie and I have become closer. She's like a favourite niece—the one who is always there when you need her. She has gone out of her way to help keep Neil's memory alive—like in 2015 when she rappelled down the Shaw Tower in Vancouver to raise funds for the Outward Bound Legacy we created in his memory.

Jennie flew to Calgary to meet me, Lucy, Scott, and a few friends, at the funeral home to view Neil's body. She went back a week later to collect his ashes and carry them on her lap to Vancouver when she came for the Vancouver memorial.

It was Jennie who joined me in Alberta in early July to meet all the wonderful RCMP officers whose voices I had come to know over those first terrible days. They arranged for two of the Parks Canada rescue crew to take us up in the same helicopter that had transported Neil's body to Canmore and retrace the journey Neil had dreamed of completing. I carried a large plastic bag filled with fresh rose petals—a gift from a mother who had met me at the Calgary airport early that morning. Her son, Brett Carlson, was an extreme skier and friend of Neil's who had died performing a skiing stunt in Whistler in January 2000.

The day was exquisitely beautiful, clear, and sunny. The Parks Canada warden shouted beneath the metallic thrumming of helicopter blades while he pointed down to the Balfour Hut and the ridge the men had followed on Neil's last day. The pilot hovered above the place from where they had staged the evacuation of my son's body, and then rose up to set the helicopter down at the edge of the ridge he had skied over, allowing us to climb out. Looking down from our icy ledge, we sat in silence releasing the rose petals onto the quiet white wilderness. We held each other and wept.

## CREATING THE NEIL FALKNER OUTWARD BOUND LEGACY

In September, five months after Neil died, a plaque was mounted on House Rock, next to the roaring Cheakamus River in Whistler. A fellow ski patroller, dressed in full Scottish regalia, played the bagpipes atop the Rock as the river rushed by. The first of many tributes, it was also the beginning of a conversation about creating a lasting legacy in his memory.

In his early teen years, Neil bounced between Toronto where his dad and brother lived, and Vancouver, where I lived with Lucy and my partner Janet. On one of our visits to Toronto, fifteen-year-old Neil told Janet and me that he wanted to return to Vancouver to live with us permanently. He was afraid to tell his dad. Janet was an awesome parental support for me and a trusted confidant for my children. She took the reins and insisted Neil should not have to deal with his father—we were the adults. Janet and I are no longer partners, but I will forever love her for that and for the support she provided when Neil died. She loved him.

Neil moved to Vancouver in time to start tenth grade at Britannia Secondary School in East Vancouver. He made new friendships, got engaged in skating and running, and seemed to be adapting well. His report cards and our visits to parent-teacher nights told a different story. Janet said, "He needs to go to Outward Bound." I hadn't heard of it before then.

We sent him on a three-week Outward Bound wilderness journey in the mountains north of Keremeos. He was sixteen, and he didn't really want to go, but that journey taught him survival was up to him. It inspired a new confidence, courage, a love of the mountains, wilderness and powder snow, and a desire to push his limits. That opportunity to connect with himself and change the way he dealt with others gave him his first taste of leadership within a guided, safe environment. Over those demanding weeks, he began to transform some of the patterns and beliefs he had about himself, and he returned home with a renewed sense of his own potential.

Did he come back Mr. Perfect? Well, he still got into trouble driving my car too fast and not finishing a geography project. He had to repeat eleventh grade social studies as well. But what he learned about himself on that journey stayed with him. In time, it took him to Whistler where he found his fit with other adventurous young people.

Neil worked for an equipment rental business and did odd jobs in summer. In winter he skied and did volunteer ski patrol until he became a pro ski patroller and avalanche safety expert on Whistler Mountain. In the last years of his life, he was passionate about developing conflict resolution skills. We would practice together whenever we had a personal clash. And as he grew into a skilled mountaineer, he called frequently to just talk and remind me, "Sending me to Outward Bound was the best thing you ever did for me."

Within ten months of his death, the Neil Falkner Outward Bound Legacy had been established, making challenging Outward Bound wilderness journeys available to deserving youth at Britannia Secondary School in East Vancouver. By 2006, we managed to raise enough to send youth from Britannia and Mount Currie, a First Nations community north of Whistler. Neil's gift continues to benefit two young people every year. By the summer of 2018, Neil's Legacy has provided twenty-nine students with my son's challenge. They're not youth with the highest grades, the strongest leadership, the best athletes, or the most confidence in themselves. They are youth, girls and boys in equal numbers, who may have to stay home and look after their siblings. They are youth who have been bullied or who have had to repeat grades. They are also LGBTQ youth. And now that I am living in Gibsons, British Colombia, they are also Sunshine Coast youth

I wonder how Neil would feel knowing that so many deserving young people have benefited from the opportunity that challenged and changed his life so many years ago. And mine too—Outward Bound sent me on a guest expedition in 2004. I understand what he meant when he said it was the best thing I ever did for him.

I go back to the memory box from time to time—to nuzzle his Whistler ski patrol fleece, to look through his photographs, and to pore over the album filled with memories and tributes. I leaf through his journal and am moved by his expressions. "I should talk to Mom about this" touches me and takes me back to the trust and camaraderie we developed over his last few years.

At Christmas, Neil's stocking is brought to the family gathering.

New messages are added to its bulk along with gratitude for all he gave us in his life and since his death. And always there is the Boursin cheese—at least one soft creamy round for the Christmas table, a ritual Neil started and we continue. This year's empty cheese box will be imbued with new tributes and will replace last year's and so on it goes.

The Marge Simpson Pez dispenser still holds a few of the tiny pastels. Do recipients of his legacy even know what a Pez dispenser is? Or who Homer and Marge Simpson are? I do know they are grateful for new courage and a new belief in themselves. That is abundantly clear from their messages of gratitude tenderly tucked in the memory box each year.

That makes me deeply grateful for birthing Neil and for the life he lived so fully.

Neil Douglas Falkner, 17 September 1969 – 12 April 2002
neilfalknerlegacy.ca

# 15.
## When David Was Killed

RANDIE CLARK

I HAD JUST RETURNED HOME from a meeting on an ordinary Wednesday evening. It was December thirteenth. Much to my delight, there was a voice mail from my son David who lived in another state with his wife. In his message, he was cheerfully telling me how relieved, excited, and happy they were about the new apartment they had just moved into. He thanked me for sending him his savings bonds, which had made it possible for them to pay the move-in costs. Their first child was due to be born in two months, and it was a relief to hear they had found a place to call home. The last words my son spoke on the recording were "I love you mom. I'll try to call you later." I then sat down with my fifteen-year-old daughter to watch our favourite trash television show about rich high school kids.

Just before 10:00 p.m., the phone rang. My daughter ran upstairs to answer it. She shouted to me to come to the phone telling me it was David's close friend calling. I remember feeling alarmed because he had never called me before. With a deep uneasiness clutching my innards I asked him "What's up?" He responded in a flat, emotionless tone, "David was robbed tonight, and there was a knife, and he was stabbed, and he's dead."

In a flash, I experienced a strange feeling surging through my body; everything froze as if the molecules of air around me had thickened and solidified. It felt as if the world had ceased to turn on its axis. I remember my vision shifting: the scene around me became surreal. The words he spoke bounced off my brain, and I could not remember what he had said. I asked, "What ... what did you say?" I forced him to repeat his words over and over. I asked him, "Why are you saying this to me?" It made no sense that he would say such a terrible thing to me. My mind raced, and my hearing was deafened by the pounding of my heart. I thought *this must be some kind of sick joke*. But no matter how many times I asked him to repeat himself, his words would not change. I demanded to speak to my daughter-in-law hoping that she would stop the hoax and free me from the terrible images flooding my mind. In the seeming eternity it took her to come to the phone, I stood frozen, and I looked across the kitchen and saw my daughter crouching in the corner repeating over and over "No, not David, not my brother." I felt utterly helpless, utterly paralyzed. When I heard my son's wife on the phone, my hopes surged; I was hungry for relief from the unfolding nightmare. She uttered, "I'm so sorry." Those words and the tone in her voice broke through my disbelief and pierced my brain. What felt like a searing hot knife plunged into my heart and forced my breath out of my body.

In that instant, the world before me shattered into swirling jagged particles. From somewhere far off, I could hear my own terrible screaming. Time stretched out, and then froze, and I lost all sensation in my body except a searing, crushing pain in my heart. I could see my daughter across the room, curled up in a ball, her eyes pleading, her voice wailing. I was helpless to stanch her pain. I felt weightless, disembodied; my field of vision narrowed to a tunnel surrounded by a swirling mass, as if I were looking into the centre of a tornado. Then in a brilliant flash, I saw a threshold before me that crossed over into a soft caress of peace, silence, and painlessness. I knew in every cell of my being that it held the promise of being with my son—all the pain and horror I was facing would end if I were to simply step across it. With every part of me longing to disappear from existence, I moved toward its magnetic pull.

My next awareness was my daughter grabbing my shoulders and shouting, "Don't leave me mom, I'm here, I won't leave you, I need you mom." In that brief moment, I faced two crystal-clear choices: step across to oblivion or stay and face the reality that my twenty-six-year-old son was dead. My daughter's voice pulled me back from the precipice. I reached toward her and life. I knew there was no turning back; we clung to each other and wailed.

Although I had no information about what had happened, in the hours following the phone call, my mind was flooded with vivid images of my son's death scene. Waves of crushing pain and helplessness swept over me. I couldn't make sense out of the most ordinary, or make simple decisions, or orient spatially. What I remember most clearly was an intense compulsion to see my son and touch him. I had to have proof he was dead. I wanted to kiss him and make it better.

It was a five-hour drive to the city where David was murdered. Upon arrival in the dawning hours, we met with the detective in charge of the homicide case who escorted me to the morgue to view my son's body. I was told I could not touch him because his body was evidence in a crime. Seeing him lying there in a body bag with only his face exposed was a moment that will be frozen in time forever. All my hope that I would awaken from a nightmare was dashed to shards. I understood his life was stopped forevermore.

As time passed, more details about his death came to light. I was obsessed with knowing each one. I was in a constant state of vigilance. Somehow it helped me feel as if I were doing something to help my son—to validate his existence. There was the arrest of the three assailants, court hearings, the coroner's report and police investigation reports, memorial gatherings, receiving David's ashes, trials, and sentencing hearings. A seemingly unending swirl of harsh and painful experiences occupied my next twelve months. Although I had hoped the end of the trials would bring some relief, I only felt sadness. My son's murderers were barely eighteen years old, and they were given life sentences with a minimum of thirty-two years before parole. Their impulsive and selfish choices had taken not only my son's life but their lives, and their families' lives were forever changed as well. It was all such a terrible waste.

No matter how much information I gathered, I could not understand why my son was dead. I continued to be haunted with movielike flashbacks—seeing him struggle for his life, falling to the ground, dying. Each time it happened, I felt as though I was right back at the beginning. The pain in my heart was relentless. At night, my mind raced through the minutia of our life together, and I looked for the mistake I made that led to his dying. I believed it was my fault; I had failed as a mother to keep my child alive. When I could sleep, I was tortured with nightmares. For the first month, I could not concentrate enough to drive a car; the world was surreal, without gravity or substance. Reading was impossible. The slightest loud noise would send my nervous system into complete alarm; I couldn't bear bright colours, the sight of knives, loud voices, or the wail of sirens. I began to shut down. I was barely functioning, exhausted, and deeply depressed. I thought I had lost my mind and sometimes contemplated my own death as a reprieve from the pain. The world around me had dimmed to shades of grey, and my feelings of shame deepened to the point that I had difficulty being in the company of others.

It was my therapist who told me that I was severely dysthymic and likely struggling with PTSD. I'd heard the term before, but I thought it was something that only soldiers had to deal with. Desperate for help, I met with a psychiatrist who specialized in traumatic loss. and he prescribed medication. I attended a support group with other survivors of homicide loss. Through sharing stories and supportive guidance came the realization that I was not alone. I learned that above and beyond my profound grief, I was experiencing symptoms of trauma injury, and with treatment and time, I could get better. Although nothing would ever bring my son back, I could regain my ability to grieve him in healthy ways.

As the symptoms I had been experiencing softened and colours returned to the world, I could begin my journey of grief in earnest. The birth of his son, my first grandchild, shone a light of hope for the future. Through rituals and gatherings, we were able to acknowledge David and to honour the place he holds in our hearts. We allowed ourselves to talk about him, to cry together, and to remember what he brought to our lives. Piece by piece, we built a new relationship with him: one of memory and love. In therapy, I learned to understand how my body and mind had been overcome by the trauma, and I learned how to help myself through loving patience, meditation, and acknowledging that his death was not my fault. The words of a friend helped me to reframe: "David did not die because you were a bad mother. He died because an idiot murdered him." His words were so simple, yet so profound.

As I began to regain a foothold, I wanted to know more about the impact of trauma on the human psyche. I immersed myself in pursuing a graduate degree in psychology. I wanted to pay forward the support and guidance that helped to save my life and sanity. And I wanted to give meaning to David's life and death by learning how to help others through the darkness and despair of grief and trauma. I will be ever grateful for the gift of witnessing others as they walk their journey of grief toward healing and finding new meaning in their lives.

It has been twenty-two years since David was murdered, and since his death, my life has changed entirely. At first, I just had to survive, to keep going, and to help my daughter. There were times when I did not believe I could live through it. Sometimes now the feelings are as raw and intense as they were that night. Sometimes I can feel deep gratitude and love toward my son for the gift of grace he has brought to my life and for awakening to the beauty of this present moment and the depth of love it holds. Not a day passes that I do not think of him and miss his quirky wit, his loving nature, and his beautiful blue eyes. I can now look back on that time with deep sadness touched with bittersweet gratitude for the twenty-six years we were blessed with his presence in our lives. And I am deeply grateful for my husband's quiet, calm support and his willingness to keep our family going through the worst of it all. To my daughter, who reached out to me from across the abyss and pulled me back toward life, I have everlasting gratitude. Witnessing her growth from a devastated young teen to a deeply spiritual and loving person leaves me in awe of the human spirit.

I will always miss my son, yet in his own way, he touches our lives every day.

# 16.
# What I Never Knew

ANTOINE BABINSKY

IN THE AFTERNOON OF 7 August 2013, as I was cutting the grass, I watched my son Michaël leaving the house on his way to the local gym where he had a part-time job as a fitness instructor. Moving at a fast pace, consumed by his thoughts as if he were visualizing how the shift was going to unfold, he looked at me briefly, waved goodbye, and then left in his car. This scene will always be imprinted in my mind, since it was the last time I saw my eldest son alive.

Thirty hours later, police informed us that they had found his body. Michaël had taken his life at twenty-three years old. I am deeply saddened my last encounter with Michaël was polite but nothing more. I had barely acknowledged his goodbye because that morning we had argued over a broken screen door. Although I now cherish the times I expressed to him I loved him, it is of small comfort in dealing with regrets and guilt for the rest of my life.

I was a senior executive in a police organization, and my wife was working as a professional in the finance department of a local university. We had great careers and were convinced that we were contributing positively to society. Both our sons, Michaël and Mathieu, were attending university. Michaël had just completed his first year of a master's of science degree and had just been awarded a prestigious national research grant (NSERC), while Mathieu was starting a chartered accounting graduate program. Although some days were not a bed of roses, we were what I considered a happy family and felt blessed for our health and happiness. We were part of a great community and lived in a friendly neighbourhood.

Michaël was an athletic, a charismatic, and an intelligent young man. He exuded self-confidence and was admired by his peers, extended family, and both his younger brother and parents. Though very talented, Michaël remained humble and always made time for his many friends and acquaintances. He was biting into life as if there was no tomorrow, and in retrospect, I wonder if this feeling unconsciously fuelled his need to accomplish so much in so little time.

Our descent into hell began with the sound of our door bell in the early hours of 9 August 2013. Two police officers were at the door. They informed my wife and me that they were investigating a death and wanted to confirm that Michaël lived with us. After establishing without a doubt the body found was my son's, I had to tell Michaël's younger brother, Mathieu, that his only brother was dead. To this day, I find it difficult to accept that destiny made me the bearer of such terrible news to my loved ones. We are led to believe bad things are not supposed to happen to good people. Unfortunately, I abruptly came to learn I don't have as much control over my life as I thought. Still stunned by the events, I had no idea how much pain was to come.

Once the police investigation was over, Mathieu, my wife, and I were told that Michaël had been suffering, unbeknown to us, from severe clinical depression. Taking medication for a few months did not sufficiently alleviate his unbearable pain and distress; he took his life without giving us any warning. That he did not confide in me, my wife, or Mathieu about his condition and that I did not pick up any signs of my son's distress will remain my ultimate failure as a parent.

Although I was devastated by our loss and was trying to make sense of what was happening, the following days were filled with difficult decisions concerning arrangements for his funeral and celebration of life. Throughout this painful ordeal, we had the support of a counsellor from my workplace employee assistance program. It turned out to be precious help while we dealt with all the bureaucratic processes and related logistics. Early in the first week, we sought guidance from a clinical psychologist who provided significant comfort as well. We also relied on the support from Mathieu's girlfriend who took notes and ensured that we ate and did not forget any tasks and arrangements concerning Michaël's celebration of life.

During these demanding times, we established a simple rule: we did not discuss or make decisions about the funeral or the estate after 7:00 p.m. This pause forced us to seek distractions such as walks, reading, and watching television. It became a period of temporary relief and created some illusion of normalcy. It had a soothing effect, which made us more receptive to a few hours of sleep induced by alcohol or medication. Since the initial visit from the police, I was having significant trouble sleeping. For the first time in my life, I had to rely on medication in order to function and navigate through the maze of funeral preparations and the array of paperwork.

Following my son's death, I noticed that my short-term memory was considerably affected, and although I have seen some improvements over the years, I still experience memory lapses. I suspect that the shock of losing a child can be similar to posttraumatic stress disorder experienced by military and first-responder personnel.

For a period of over six months, I found I could not stand in the front lobby of my home late at night without experiencing severe stress and anxiety. The lighting produced at that time of night made me relive all the emotions I felt when police entered my home on that dramatic night.

Initially, when responding to the police officers investigating my son's death, I was in work mode and naturally took the lead in liaising with the authorities. However, after my assistance was no longer required, I broke down lying on the floor of my son's bedroom, hugging his dirty laundry in a last attempt to feel his presence. Since then, I have cried a river. Although I know I am progressively healing, I continue to be very sensitive to anything emotional and that easily brings tears to my eyes.

As a senior executive, I was used to conducting meetings involving a large number of people, but after the event, I could no longer attend even an informal gathering with more than four friends. It took a few years for me to feel comfortable again in larger crowds.

The tragic event amplified my introvert personality to the point of avoiding contact with everyone except immediate relatives or friends who insisted on meeting my wife and me. Although we missed many close friends, we could not find the strength to initiate the first steps to get together, as we knew it could jeopardize the relationship. Often we cancelled at the last minute because we just did not feel comfortable in social gatherings.

Meeting people or even making phone calls seemed like enormous tasks, which kept draining all the limited energy we had. I would put out the garbage in the early morning hours just to minimize contact with neighbours, despite knowing how supportive they had been. Any simple chore generating trivial complications became difficult to manage, and created abnormal anxiety and frustration. To this day, I feel something is broken inside of me. I feel much more vulnerable, and I am learning to accept my new reality.

I can say now that deciding to stop taking sleeping pills shortly after Michaël's celebration of life was a mistake. Although I was concerned about developing an addiction, I found myself over-compensating by drinking copious quantities of alcohol to relax, especially in the evening. I have since drastically reduced my alcohol consumption, but I realize consulting a health practitioner would have been a wise decision.

Facing such despair, I came to realize my only way to survive was to go back to basics. Although it may seem simplistic or corny, having sufficient sleep, maintaining a balanced diet, and exercising made an enormous difference in gaining stamina to deal with my loss. It might be because of the nature of Michaël's death, but I still carry a lot of anger inside of me. At times, I have had thoughts of breaking furniture and walls in my house but always found enough restraint and common sense not to do so. I can honestly say that exercise such as swimming has helped me manage that anger and frustration.

As I am writing these lines, I hardly remember who came to the funeral home and to the church for the celebration of life because of my state of numbness. Besides a general thank-you notice in the local newspapers, my wife and I have not yet found the strength or the courage to go through the funeral home registry and send personal thank-you cards to everyone for their compassion and support during those especially hard times. Although it bothers us at times, we are trying not to feel guilty over procrastination and to accept that there will be things we will never be able to do.

The consequences of not accomplishing some of the things on the wish list can never be worse than losing our beloved son. If some friends or relatives are offended by Mathieu, my wife, or me for omitting to do something in a timely fashion, they are simply not worth our emotional investment.

My wife recently reminded me of how our relationship with time has significantly changed since the beginning of this nightmare. In some instances, it feels like an eternity when waiting for something or accomplishing a task, while, at other times, when left to our thoughts and memories, hours seem to fly by in a matter of minutes.

I now have this distinct perception that my life can be divided in two: the first portion being the happy, naïve period prior to Michaël's passing and the second part beginning with the tragedy and filled with sorrow, pain, and darkness. I would give every-thing to go back to those happier times so as not to belong to the circle of parents who have lost a child. I truly miss the feeling of joy and lightness you get when you realize how fortunate you are and how wonderful life can be. I strongly wish that mindset could come back. Of course, since Michaël's passing, I have experienced many superficial pleasures, but I can never enjoy anything for long before I come to my senses and realize that my son is gone and I will never be able to share these moments with him.

Although I had just started my retirement and had no pressure to be back at work, my wife was on sick leave for sixteen months. What got us on the road to recovery were the numerous conver-sations we had with a former colleague of mine who had also lost a son the year before our loss. She knew the pain we were experiencing, and our discussions made us realize we were not going crazy and the changes and challenges we were going through were normal. This was further confirmed by our attendance at many support group meetings organized by our local chapters of Bereaved Families of Ontario and Compassionate Friends. We quickly came to understand that grief is a journey with many ups and downs and that it is perfectly natural to sometimes feel we are regressing.

Revealing specifics about how we felt and how we were living our grief with others experiencing similar pain helped us under-stand what we had to expect in the future. My wife and I came to develop bonds with some of these parents who became as close or closer to us than some family members.

The most important thing was that sharing personal anecdotes or observations about our grieving process came as a relief to me. It took a load off my shoulders. Peers and coaches provided us with tools to help us through our journey and gave us hope we would eventually feel better. In one of the support groups, I wrote a short letter to Michaël and read it to my peers. The exercise was difficult, but it helped me progress tremendously. We borrowed the idea of lighting a candle at supper time. Its soft light brings us peace and comfort in thinking Michaël is with us. To this day, we continue to light a candle at supper time.

I also learned it is much easier to occupy your mind with work or a hobby than setting time aside to deal with your loss. But although it is painful to deal with emotions, I had to live through them in order to progress through such difficult grief. I now feel more confident I can manage my life better—to the point of helping others with similar grief. The support meetings have allowed me to interact with parents who lost a child long before I had. They have given me hope that one day I will wake up without my first thought being "Michaël is no longer with us" and that I will not think of Michaël every minute, every hour, and every day. By then, when I think of my beloved departed son, it won't be of the circumstances around his death, but more about the many tender and joyful moments we spent together.

At the beginning, Michaël's passing took all the space in my life. However, as I proceeded through my grieving and started to live different experiences, strengthening relationships and making new friends, these events started giving meaning and purpose to my life.

It is true that the pain is not as acute as years go by; nevertheless, it is always present. For the first while, I had no desire or energy to seek the pleasures life can offer. I felt empty and nothing mattered except my surviving son. In the darkest days, my only reason to survive revolved around Mathieu who deserved more than ever his parents' attention and devotion. I realize that my lifeline is dependent on the wellbeing of my child, and I don't know how I could survive another loss similar to the one I am going through. Although I had no specific reason to worry about Mathieu's safety,

I was afraid of losing him too, and I became hypervigilant. Any phone call or ring of the doorbell after regular hours made my heart pound. I am less worried now, but I no longer take wellbeing for granted as I used to.

Before Michaël's passing, I could not imagine how it felt to lose a child. I still recall having a business meeting with a colleague who had lost a son. Although I was not close to that person, I never brought up the topic, as I thought it would create unnecessary tension or could trigger unwanted emotions during the course of our professional encounter. Sadly enough, it never came to my mind that inquiring how that person was doing when dealing with such a loss could have been a welcomed acknowledgment and a true sign of caring. Obviously, I would now do things differently.

Although I admit it is a daily struggle, I try not to interpret the awkwardness and silence of my friends as a lack of compassion. I forgive all my acquaintances, friends, and relatives who avoid talking about Michaël or our loss; they no doubt think it would hurt us. Instead, we worry they are forgetting him. How I wish people would understand how devastating and painful it is to lose a child. For many, including myself, our upbringing has failed to provide us with sufficient tools to deal with death and the grieving of friends and relatives.

I realize it may not be what people feel comfortable doing, but talking about Michaël brings me great joy and great comfort. For me, it simply means he is still alive and the impact of his presence and his actions are still felt and ultimately matter. In bringing up Michaël in a conversation, I must have upset some people, but others have said they felt more at ease and closer to me.

Although it appeared at times that Mathieu did not want to deal with grieving for his older brother, I realized with time that siblings manage their loss differently than parents. Mathieu has kept more to himself and will not often discuss his brother with us; perhaps, he is afraid he could be hurting us. I have learned to accept that his grieving process can be as good as mine.

Even though I understand there is no malicious intent, I often feel people believe that after several years, bereaved parents should be over their grieving and ready to move on. Nothing is further from the truth. But how can I make someone understand that losing a child is the worst thing that can happen to someone. It is a life sentence I can never be released from; I will feel its impact until I die.

Currently, my biggest fear is forgetting things about Michaël. Although I am his father and was at his side for most of his life, I fear time will slowly erode memories of him and the process will be even faster among relatives and friends. Like many bereaved parents, I have felt the urge to plant trees and to frame pictures and memorabilia. I got a tattoo to ensure I have constant reminders of his time on this earth.

We did not know what to do with our son's belongings. Our first reaction was to gather everything in his room and not touch anything. Over time, I came to realize that keeping all his personal effects is not what Michaël would have wanted. To ensure that his memory remains alive within our more intimate circle, we have started to give his belongings away to his friends and relatives. It is while grieving that these belongings will mean the most to them—having a piece of Michaël by their side when faced with the challenges of young adult life.

At every anniversary of Michaël's passing, I have been torn between participating in some kind of commemoration or simply not doing anything. Although my wife has expressed the desire to be part of an activity centred around Michaël that day, I have trouble doing it. I cannot come to terms with making this day special when it was the worst day of my life. My wish has always been not to see anyone on that day and to occupy my mind with activities that do not remind me of my loss. I can't wait for the day to be over; I feel relief when the week, the month, and even the season reminding me of my son's death are behind me. I believe any commemoration should be done on his birthday. We have done so by sharing a meal and anecdotes with his friends.

The third anniversary of Michaël's passing was particularly difficult for me to try to ignore and just get through. In past years, the pain was mixed with numbness. This time, my brain seemed to clearly understand my son is dead. Michaël is not away travelling; he is not at school or at work. He is gone forever. I will never feel again his strong handshake. I will never witness his contagious laughter or talk with him about training, sports, real estate, or his future. I don't think I will ever accept that situation. I am trying to learn how to live without him, but it is still very hard to do.

I cling to the belief that Mathieu, my wife and I will be reunited with Michaël one day.

"Our love, our shooting star."

# 17.
# Four Poems

LAURA APOL

## The Little Mermaid
## by Edvard Eriksen
*Copenhagen, April 23, 2017*

Such eyes
        as she studies the water.
In four days, she will trade so much.

She knows how it will be:
    a sword through the body.

      She can never go
      home.

Soon, she will be only foam
        on memory's sea.

*Oh, daughter—*

      I would touch your smooth cheek,
stroke your hair. Birth you,
        again and again.

—but for the ocean between us.
But for the rocks.

## Then Come the Dreams

of what I must do
        and do over

      —*bury my daughter. Bury my daughter.*
I wake in a panic,

but it is already done. It has been done
      for so long—
all her life, leaving
        a trail of ash

that shows
where my heart
        has been.


## First Mother's Day
## After Her Death

Before dawn, I jolt
      from a labyrinth dream—

        she is lost
        at the center
no matter my search. *Who can reach her?*

We used to go for mother-daughter
pedicures;

now paper-white trillium
        bloom where she stood.

All day,
    I circle
    the space in me
        that was her.

## Patient Stone

*In Iran, we have a tradition to help with grief. It involves a "patient stone." When your pain is too overwhelming, you wander the fields in search of your patient stone. Once you find it, you sit alone and tell it your story. With each word and each sentence, your pain is supposed to lessen until you completely unburden yourself. You know you have reached the end when the stone bursts into pieces.*

Amir,
        I would like to believe
in your patient stone. All afternoon
                I have searched.

I think it is not so much
        that I will find it—
it will find me.

But
there is much
                I do not understand.

How large is a stone
that can manage this work?

Do I visit it, broken?
Do I carry it home?

I will need
        the right stone. We will be life
companions.

We will share one heart.

# 18.
# Randy

BONNIE HARDY

*Everything that has happened to me—took place through
some agreement— made in pre-eternity.*

—Hafiz

IN 1966, I BEGAN MY cross-Canada trip to Gander, Newfoundland. I had been hoping to see Canada via train, before flying to
Britain to begin a year of backpacking through Europe. My plans,
however, were interrupted by a train strike. In lieu of the train, I
checked the bulletin board at the University of Alberta and read,
"Looking for a ride east? Student with Volkswagen looking to
share driving and expenses." We traded drivers every few hours
and slept when not at the wheel. Amazing what twenty-one-year-
olds can do.

We arrived in Toronto on the morning of day three. It was Labour
Day weekend, and the Snowbirds were performing that afternoon.
Hotels and youth hostels were full. I was alone, standing on the
sidewalk, exhausted, and crying. Opening my address book, I
found the contact number of a woman I had worked with in the
sociology department. I phoned, and she was quick to invite me
to stay. By the time I reached their apartment I was in a terrible
state of sobbing and collapse. The two women assisted me up the
stairs to their home. I fell soundly asleep. The following morning,
I was determined to keep heading east, and I declined my friend's
invitation to stay another night.

I found a ride to Québec City. But the whole day, as we travelled
east, I would turn around and look behind me because I had the

unsettling image of a rifle constantly in my mind's eye.

I arrived at the Gander Ferry Terminal at 10:00 p.m. and was told there was an urgent RCMP message asking me to phone home to Edmonton. Fearing that something had happened to my father, I telephoned: my thirteen-year-old brother, Randy, had fallen from a cliff and died. My parents had taken Grandma, Randy, and his friend Michael on a Labour Day weekend fishing trip. The ferry cashier took me, sobbing, home with her. Sometime in the night, I awoke yelling "He's here! He's here!" Randy was talking to me in my dreams.

After flying back to Edmonton, my grandmother's first question was "Did you know?" She and I were redheads and thought to be intuitive. I said I had been crying constantly for three days but did not know why. On a cellular level, three generations of my family had been grief stricken and sobbing with a distance of two thousand miles between us.

Later, talking to my older sister, I explained, "The whole day I travelled east to Québec City, I kept looking behind me because there was a constant image of a rifle in my mind. I wonder why that particular symbol of death shadowed me as I travelled."

"Oh," she replied. "I think I might know. When you were three years old, we were visiting Gram at the farm. Uncle Jim, who was fifteen at the time, was cleaning his rifle when it accidently went off, and the bullet buzzed past you. Mom yelled "You almost killed her! You could have killed her!" That incident was consciously unknown to me, but it had manifested on a subconscious level.

When I heard the story of Randy's fall and how my father had descended into the valley to carry Randy's body out, I was told my father met two First Nations men, who carried Randy for him. My father's emotions then took over and he collapsed.

I believe I was in that state at the same moment in time, but miles away, when I reached my friend's home in Toronto, they needed to come outside and carry me up the stairs to bed.

In reality, I had to keep going east to Gander while my parents returned home from their Labour Day weekend trip so that I could be recognized and stopped at the Gander Ferry Terminal. The RCMP had put out an all-points bulletin, but my only known destination was the Gander Ferry Terminal.

On several occasions in Trevor's young life, I wondered if my son was the reincarnation of my little brother Randy. In our 1954 family photos, I was often seen feeding my two-year-old baby brother. In other photos, I'm holding a glass of milk to his lips, spoon feeding him, or taking him to the park to swing. At nine years of age, I was his "little mother": I cared for him at meals and took him with me as we explored our neighbourhood.

Thirty years later, as mother of three-year-old Trevor and seven-month-old Brendan, we rode the Vancouver Island train from Victoria to Parksville to visit my parents. Our conductor announced, "look to your right, we will be crossing the Koksilah River Canyon Trestle bridge; 188 metres long and 38 metres high." Everyone on the train stood up and moved to the right side of the train to peer down into the canyon; three-year-old Trevor yelled "Sit down! You'll fall!" This and other incidents piqued my curiosity. Could my firstborn son be the reincarnation of my little brother Randy who had died by falling?

### TREVOR: THE DEATH I NEVER SAW COMING

My mother's death had been revealed to me in multiple dreams over an entire year, but this was not the case for my son's death. Trevor himself had precognitive images. He told me that the raw images of the 9/11 crashes on the news resembled his recurring dream where he was pinned down while he attempted to extricate himself, smoke and fire all around him.

Trevor's journey to a new plane of existence began at 6:30 p.m. 20 December 2005. I did not learn of it until midnight when my sons Brendan and Douglas arrived with the police. I was told Trevor's plane had crashed during takeoff from Terrace B.C. at 6:30 p.m. Terrace Police first contacted Nav Air for pilot names and next of kin, and then contacted local Victoria RCMP.

Devastating news. Douglas, Brendan, and I held one another and sobbed and cried, tears streaming. I have been told that hours later I tucked my adult sons into bed saying a prayer over them. "Now I lay me down to sleep, I pray the Lord my soul to keep." The words arose from my childhood as I prayed that all my sons be safe.

Trevor the firstborn: the one who was photographed endlessly, the child who changed our lives from lovers to parents, the child whose routine had each subsequent child pulled out of bed to race Trevor, the firstborn, off to kindergym, hockey practice, drum lessons, or a play date. The child who was a miracle! How could we lose him so soon?

The following day I was sleep deprived and feeling comatose from shock and grief when my friend Barb arrived. She and I had both lost brothers as children. Our children had been in French Immersion together. Barb stayed by my side all day. When the 5:00 p.m. news was about to come on she quietly informed me that I had a decision to make. I could watch the news knowing it may remain forever in my psyche as trauma, or I could not watch the news knowing I may regret never having viewed it.

I watched the newscast of my firstborn son's horribly tragic demise. The cockpit, with its two precious pilots, was destroyed. The cargo had survived, scattered over the snowy forest floor.

Although I do remember Barb's presence, I'm told that my niece, my sister, my high school friends, and neighbours were also here that day, bringing flowers, food, and condolences. I recall none of that. I have only an awareness of Barb's presence beside me while I grieved within a cocoon of emotional upheaval. Numb, I never felt hunger. I lost twenty pounds over the coming months.

On 22 December 2005, Chek TV interviewed Douglas, Brendan, and me. Brendan was angry and made comments regarding the reputation of the thirty-year-old MU2 cargo plane and its history of multiple deadly crashes during landing or takeoff, which give it the reputation among pilots as the widow maker. After the news broadcast, Trevor's friends gathered at our home. Neighbours, friends and family arrived with food, condolences, tears, and many fun Trevor stories.

Nav Air pilots brought a video made in honour of two other young Nav Air pilots who had perished in a fiery plane crash on the tarmac in Nanaimo, just seven months earlier. The cause was a ten dollar plug, a knock off that was not heat resistant. As pilot and weather man for Nav Air, Trevor had been the last person to speak to colleagues Wesley and Geoff.

We all gathered around the TV to view the video of a cargo

pilot's daily routine. The film began at 6:00 a.m. with a dark and rainy departure from the Vancouver airport. But soon we watched images of blue cloudless skies, sunshine, glistening snowy mountain peaks and the caption: "It's a beautiful view from the office today!" Trevor preferred the Penticton-Kelowna route, which was warm and dry upon landing, as opposed to the snow and cold they met on the Smithers-Terrace route. We all cried while watching *A Day in the Life of a Cargo Pilot*.

Suddenly, thunder and lightning struck the front lawn of our two-acre farm. Frightened, we rushed outside in awe of the blinding light and thunderous rumblings. We felt Trevor was not happy with his unexpected and too-soon transformation.

As I entered the kitchen, I was directly facing a tall man in a white tuxedo and tails. His shoulders were too wide and flat; his tuxedo jacket and tails extended to his knees. I walked over to shake the young man's hand, and introduced myself as Trevor's mother. When I asked "How did you know my son," Tuxedo man's head went back, and his jaw dropped in surprise! Trying to fill the awkward silence, I asked, "Did you go to school with Trevor?" Again his head went back, his mouth open in surprise. At this point, a young woman leaned forty-five degrees sideways, out from behind him, and murmured "Oh around—just around." She too was dressed all in white and had long blonde ringlets. Later when I described this mysterious encounter, a friend suggested "his angel?" There is a belief that someone from the other side meets us when we cross over.

Unsuccessful in engaging tuxedo man in conversation, I turned to ask the Nav Air Pilots if they knew who this person could be. We turned to look. The man in white had vanished. I asked others, but no one had seen him except me. Although he was much taller than Trevor (I had to look up to make eye contact), I am now certain that this angelic being was Trevor, present among us, and attending his final gathering. I was the only person to see him, and he was clearly astonished that I could see him.

Scott arrived asking to do the eulogy. "Trevor and I have become great friends since he moved to Vancouver." Ah! Now "funeral" had been brought to my numbed consciousness. Magic happened around us in order for a memorial service to materialize Christmas week. We felt it was important that the service be held while Trevor's friends were home for Christmas. Don offered to officiate. The First Unitarian Church was booked. Trevor's preschool teacher offered to play piano, and overnight, friends created a PowerPoint photo presentation of Trevor's short but active life. What a gift to be embraced, surrounded, and supported by friends while I sat dazed, immobile, and unbelieving.

It was eerie—the deep roots and interwoven connections of people stepping forward to offer their time and skills toward Trevor's final honouring. Volunteer singers from the Gettin' Higher Choir all knew Trevor well. A high school friend, Sue, recognized me from the television crash clip. She had no idea I was Trevor's mother. Trevor had been her new son-in-law's best man at his wedding. Her brother was Trevor's Vancouver dentist. Sue and Megan sang "Always" at Trevor's memorial.

Trevor's memorial service, on 27 December, was a roast—a space for friends to rib Trevor, tell tall tales, and share memorable stories about him. It became apparent to me that Trevor was a friend to all who knew him; he had a gift for making people feel at ease and for bringing diverse groups together. He is remembered for his fun-loving ways, infectious smile, hard-working nature, and mischievous sense of humour.

I put Trevor's photos on Facebook, and presto! Trevor's friends connected and shared up close and personal photos and stories. Trevor had been ecstatic after his first solo flight. His instructions were: "keep one wing over the land and one wing over the water along the Vancouver Island coastline from Victoria to Comox." I still remember Trevor's phone call, excited, "Oh Mum, it's amazing to view the areas I have visited all my life, but now I'm seeing them from above!" We had spent summers on Hornby and Salt Spring Islands, or hiking up Mt. Albert Edward, where the 360-degree view was just trees, with no clear cuts, telephone wires, or roads. Winters, we had holidayed at Mount Washington. Trevor had been in awe — flying over his childhood playground during his first solo flight.

After arrival at their destination, pilots would catch forty winks at a bed and breakfast during the morning. When they awoke, it was lunchtime. Afternoons, they worked out in a gym and at 5:00

p.m., they would pick up bank mail from Smithers. Once loaded, they flew back to Terrace for the 5:30 p.m. bank mail pickup, and then they headed back to Vancouver. They were gone dawn till dusk in the dark of winter.

On their last fatal flight, Trevor and Simon departed Vancouver airport at 6:00 a.m. Departing Terrace at 6:30 p.m., the MU2 burst into flames and crashed into dense forest twenty seconds after takeoff. The Terrace airport did not have fire-fighting equipment, nor could the emergency crew access to the crash site, which was over the fence, off the tarmac. The plane burned for twelve hours lighting up the sky, producing an orange glow over Terrace.

Ann, the other pilot's wife, asked that her husband's gold wedding band be returned to her, but was told it had melted in the heat.

Over the next year, we were angry after discovering the deadly history and crash statistics of the MU2. We wrote letters, called lawyers, and talked to Transport Canada. We spoke with other grieving families, parents, and spouses who had lost loved ones to the MU2. Originally an executive jet, the MU2 was converted for cargo rather than passengers. It sits low to the ground, which is great for loading cargo through a large side door. Its high wing allows the cargo area to be loaded efficiently from the tarmac rather than having to hoist cargo up a set of stairs. Cargo pilots transport bank records, medical supplies, factory parts for FedEx and UPS, holiday gifts, business letters, and scores of other products. Industry, as well as individual consumers who order products to be shipped overnight, drives air cargo. But the MU2 has a deadly secret: the plenum cracks and splits during runway activity. The high revs during takeoff and landing can open unseen cracks in the plenum, which creates a gasoline fire in the left engine. The plane yaws and spins in circles with only the right engine operating.

Trevor's father, my ex-husband, received a copy of the federal government's Draft Report of the Terrace Crash and Teardown Findings. We had been separated for seven years, so I asked for a copy, but was told "sorry, only next of kin qualify." Stunned, I sent off the following message:

"I conceived Trevor on the anniversary date of the first year of marriage to his father. I sheltered Trevor within my womb—nurturing and nourishing him for nine months. I birthed him into this world on 11 July 1974. I breast fed him for the first six months of his life. I watched him take his very first steps. I loved him intensely for thirty-one short years. I will grieve him for the rest of my days. Does this make me next of kin, and qualify me for a draft report of my son's final moments on earth?"

The report was mailed.

Over the next year, I saw Trevor everywhere. While grocery shopping, I saw him in the next aisle and quickly followed him, only to discover a Trevor lookalike. Or I saw Trevor walking down the street and thought, *oh here he is.* But it was never my son. What mysterious malady protects a mother from the full realization that her child is gone?

I could not accept the finality of Trevor's death. It wasn't until several family birthdays, Thanksgivings, and Christmases came and went that I understood and finally allowed myself to endure the full realization that Trevor had shed the "clothing" of this life. Yet my heart weeps for the hopes and dreams Trevor worked so hard to fulfill in this lifetime, and the emptiness of knowing there will be no Trevor grandbabies.

Trevor had given me an atlas the previous Christmas, so I could plan my retirement explorations and holiday journeys as the mother of a pilot. Life is intangible, fragile, and precious.

Longing for connection to Trevor, I read letters on his legacy website. I laughed remembering how little Trevor had no trouble finding a wall to ride his bike on, stairs to catapult over, someone to tease, or a pal to have an adventure with. His friends of today made it clear that this fun-loving path on the edge continued for big Trevor. So if time is measured not by the years of your life but the life in your years, then Trevor had a friend- and family-filled life indeed.

I went to see a counsellor. During the meeting, he fell asleep as I spoke to him. I began apologizing to him because he had to listen to these kinds of stories over and over again. He apologized and blamed it on having eaten too much sugar at lunchtime. Chagrined, I signed up for group counselling, but I found myself with people asking "when did you lose your husband?" I didn't fit anywhere.

I joined a hospice art therapy course. Cutting out magazine pictures for my son's memory poster board made me cry. The images were poignant and resulted in opening the tear floodgates.

But my very best therapist was our sweet, wee puppy, Shanti. She didn't walk far at first, but everyone who saw her came over to chat, and I would pour out the story of my firstborn son's death over and over and over to whomever would stop and listen.

Next, I attended a week long Gangaji Gathering in Vancouver, which allowed long held-in tears to flow relentlessly. That week I stood on a deck overlooking a garden and spotted tiny crystalline pieces sparkling at me. I began picking them up to study them. Spotting another and another, I soon had all thirty-one sparkling faceted pieces: Trevor was thirty-one. Those pieces were gathered at my most vulnerable ebb; they seemed to say "Hello Mum. I'm here. I'm okay. You'll be fine." I brought the thirty-one sparkles home in a little bag, and every once in a while, one of them will jump to freedom and lie sparkling on the floor of my bedroom—a manifestation that Trevor is still around, ever the trickster.

Trevor used to phone me at 8:30 a.m. from whatever town he was in. He was good at languages and a variety of accents. He would pretend to book a weekend getaway at my bed and breakfast, and I would bite. But by the end of the outrageous conversation, I would suddenly realize I was speaking with my trickster son.

My niece's husband, Tom, owns a busy service station in Victoria. One day after Trevor's death, all the computers in the station went down. When Tom's computer came back up, it displayed Trevor's receipt for maintenance done on his car. The hair stood up on Tom's neck. And when Trevor's friends get together for a special occasion, they tell me the Mixmaster springs to life with no one touching it.

A Salt Spring Island astrologer did a horoscope for the time of the plane crash. Planets were in an equidistant twelve-point circle, open to guide and receive Trevor and Simon.

As a friend and I walked and talked along Dallas Road shortly after Trevor's funeral, a seagull kept circling around us. It would circle then hover in my face. After its fifth circle and hover, I stopped walking, looked at my friend, and asked "this isn't just chance, is it?" The seagull circled and hovered one last time: when it knew it had our full attention, it departed with one wing over the land and one wing over the water. Thanks for saying hi, Trevor.

As the Buddha has said, "Like birds spending a night together on a tree, and going their separate directions the next morning, so inevitably the union of all beings ends in parting. As clouds coming together in the sky only to separate again, so do creatures collect together and then disperse."

# 19.
# Guess It's Time to Put it Down

BARB DUNCAN

I HAVE BEEN WRITING THIS in my head all summer. Guess it's time to put it down.

After more than forty years, I look back and see that times were very different. There were no seatbelts, driving drunk was not as socially unacceptable as it is now, and self-help groups were unheard of.

In July 1973, we were a very ordinary young family—mom, dad, two boys, Gordon ten, Andrew five, and one girl, Dana, almost eight.

Both Keith and I were working at the National Arts Centre, he in maintenance, I as a nurse. We were due to leave on holiday on the Friday of the August long weekend. Everyone wanted to be off work, and as we had no plans that could not be postponed, we agreed to work the weekend and leave on Tuesday. Not knowing what is coming is a blessing I guess. Would going on holiday as we planned have changed anything? We would always wonder.

The Queen was coming to Ottawa, and my daughter was beyond excited to see "her" Queen. On Friday, my mom took all three children to see the Queen while I worked. The boys were pretty blasé about it, but Dana couldn't stop talking about how close they were to the Queen.

Saturday was a beautiful summer day. I took the kids with me to the Arts Centre when I went to work. On the way, we stopped at the library to choose books to take on our holiday, and then we went to a craft festival at the Art Centre. The kids were fascinated by the glassblower. He told them that I had helped him when he was injured, so he made a mouse for them, and I bought a swan. After that, they attended the children's show, and I went to work. The last time I saw Dana was when she scooted back to say "Love you, Mom" and then dropped her swan on the tile floor. This was typical. Fortunately, it was well wrapped and survived.

When Keith finished work at 4:00 p.m., he picked up the kids to take them home. Shortly after that time, I received a phone call from a neighbour's daughter saying "There has been an accident, but Keith and the boys are fine, and they are just going to the hospital to be checked over." When I asked about Dana, she said that was all she had been told. I made arrangements to cover my shift and drove to the closest hospital, but they weren't there. Staff there called another hospital, and I was able to talk to Keith. He said he and the boys were okay, but he was scared for Dana, and I knew the hospital they were at meant a head injury.

When I arrived, I found the boys had minor physical scrapes, Keith had a badly injured leg, and Dana had a severe head injury. Gordon, almost ten, had been put in the first ambulance with Dana so they could send the youngest with Keith. Unfortunately, Gordon understood what was going on as they fought to keep Dana alive. He told me the driver kept using the siren and complaining because cars weren't giving them the right of way. By the time Keith got to the hospital, Gordon had given them all the information except the health insurance number.

How I wish I had known then what I know now about grief. Since that time, Gordon has been anxious of ambulances on the road, and it took many years before I realized that he felt guilty because he wouldn't give Dana the front seat of the car on the way home. She was in the back seat, and when they were hit she was directly at point of impact.

Closing my eyes, I relive that time at the hospital as if it were yesterday, and in my mind, I see the drunk driver who hit them.

I remember the nurse who grabbed a bundle of linen and walked beside Dana's stretcher as she was wheeled from the emergency room so her brothers would not see their sister with all the invasive tubes. I went to the recovery room to see her. As I was leaving, one of the older surgeons stopped and gave me a hug. I learned later he had also lost a daughter. The surgeon looking after her was noted for lack of bedside manner, but he treated me with great compassion as he explained my daughter was brain dead.

Keith and I had discussed organ transplant for ourselves but never considered it in connection with our children. Dana was cared for in the recovery room until the next day when her kidneys and corneas were removed for transplant.

When Keith and I arrived home, we told our sons their sister was dead. Holding each other as we cried was the most relief we had that night. I kept thinking I could have easily lost all four of them. We were in the midst of a nightmare, and that day felt unreal. We were doing what had to be done but almost in a trance. Our families came together around us with no idea what to do to help us. We were all exhausted but couldn't sleep.

Planning a funeral at age thirty—who knows how to plan a funeral for their child? What we didn't know. We had a closed casket, although Dana didn't have a visible injury. Most people thought this meant she was too badly hurt to be seen. And how do you explain when you can't understand yourself?

Three days later, instead of heading off on holiday, we were burying our only daughter.

We lived with a sense of unreality where grief hit us like a hammer often and at unexpected times.

After that, we went away for almost a month while Keith's leg healed. We tried to make sense of the unthinkable and, at the same time, care for our other children. Later, we often wondered what we did during that time. We became overprotective of our independent boys and needed them to be within sight all the time. This became a problem for them, and we needed some negotiations to solve that problem.

### ANGER AND TERROR

I was a nurse who had previously worked with the elderly for many years. Death was something I had often dealt with. I had read Elizabeth Kubhler-Ross's books and went back and read them again, as I looked for any help I could find. There were lots of scenarios but none regarding the loss of a young child.

My overriding emotion for the next year was anger—at God, drunk drivers, the school system, the justice system, most everyone. We told the school principal what had happened so the teachers would be prepared. The level of rage I felt when I found out that he hadn't told any of the teachers and that my children had to tell them what happened almost choked me.

When the boys were around, I bottled up my anger and carried on. I couldn't sleep, and I couldn't cry. None of us wanted to say Dana's name, yet we yearned to hear it. When I think back to that time, tears come easily.

When my husband and I went back to work, everyone treated us with kid gloves; likely, they did not know what to say or whether we would accept sympathy. But we had small children, so covering our heads and staying in bed weren't options. One day, we thought we were doing okay. The next day, the bottom dropped out, and it was back to day one again with all the devastation that entailed. Two of my friends came with hugs saying they "weren't good at this," but the hugs were the best things.

Some people said "Isn't it lucky that Andrew is too young to understand that his sister is gone?" They thought he didn't understand! More anger. Almost everything made me angry.

My mother had lost an infant girl when I was young. You might think that when my daughter died, we would have been able to connect because of that. But it didn't happen. Mom said she was afraid of saying the wrong thing and that I might fall to pieces. Instead, she hugged me often and told me we were good parents. Years later, she and I sat at her mother's grave on a warm sunny day and talked and cried about our losses. Before then, I hadn't appreciated how hard it is for a parent to grieve not only for their grandchild but their child's loss as well.

The other emotion was absolute terror that someone would say something about losing our "only girl" and the boys might misunderstand and think we would have rather lost one of them. It wasn't until our younger son was in college that this arose. He called saying he had to come home to talk to us. A girl in his sociology class mentioned that her only brother had died, and it suddenly struck him that we had lost our only girl. He said "I had never thought about that."

There were no self-help groups in those days. If you carried on, everyone assumed you were fine unless they also had a child who had died. Keith grieved differently than I did. He was a stoic man, and looking back, I think Gordon followed his dad's lead. One day that first winter Andrew crawled onto Keith's lap and said "You never cry. Don't you miss her?" We all stood there locked in a hug, sobbing uncontrollably. Then we talked about how some people were benefiting because of the organ transplants from Dana, and as young as they were, the boys found comfort in this. As time went on, we talked about her, and we encouraged the boys to talk about her. We laughed at the many escapades of our daughter, who was hyperkinetic before that was a word. We were fortunate to have family and friends who closed ranks around us until we could function on our own again. My sisters-in-law were my rocks; they were always there to listen.

Nine years later, on the anniversary of Dana's death, the unthinkable happened. A dear friend's son drowned. We passed on as much support as we could, but we were also in shock. By then, Bereaved Families of Ontario had been formed. After attending a group, my friend took the facilitator training to give back some of the help she had received. She convinced me that I should join her. Those training sessions were like reliving that time again—the shock of knowing it could happen to us and remembering that lonely time when the world as we knew it fell apart.

I found that I was quite good at facilitating, and in doing so, I was helped as much as the participants.

Over the years, I have learned this:

- Grief is physical as well as emotional.
- You never get over it; you just learn to cope better with the reality.
- Helping others is a great way to help yourself.

When the boys became teenagers they knew that the song "The Littlest Angel" made me cry. If I was driving, I had to pull over until I was in control again. One Christmas, they gave me a CD of it and a box of Kleenex. They told me I could listen to it when I chose, and the roads would be safer. Music still catches me unaware sometimes, and I am back in 1973 hearing a small voice singing.

We raised two good men who have made us proud. One son married a woman with three daughters. We had small girls in our family again. The other brought us a grandson.

Even so, in our family, the August long weekend is always an anxious time.

Reading this over, it seems very disjointed, but the reality is that life was very disjointed for many years. I would never wish this on anyone. People ask "How did you manage?" and they say they could never have survived. My answer is always the same. "No one gave us a choice." We did the best we could with what we had, and I guess that is all anyone can do.

# 20.
# Hole in My Heart

MICHELINE LEPAGE

I WANT TO SHARE MY STORY in the hope that others who have
lost a child know that the pain and emptiness never go away—
they just get more manageable.

On 20 November 2014, my son BJ (Bruce Junior) passed away.
He was only thirty-two years old.

He hadn't been feeling well since November 2013. He had been
to a walk-in clinic and been treated for pneumonia according to
the symptoms he described. On 15 February 2014, after much
persuading, he agreed to let us take him to the emergency department of the Ottawa Hospital. I am so grateful for having been with
him that day. Neither of us had any idea what awaited us, but my
motherly instinct told me something was seriously wrong. Within
two hours, after having had blood work done and an ultrasound,
the doctor told us that BJ had kidney cancer. Life drained out of
me, but I was able to find the strength to be strong for him. I tried
to calm him and told him not to make any conclusions until we
heard more from the specialists. After a while, I left the room and
let go of my emotions in the hall. Then I composed myself and
called his wife, Lori, my husband Barrie, his father-in-law Paul,
my sister Lynda, and my daughter Natalie. For the first time in
my life, I felt so powerless. As a mom, it was my job to fix things
and make things better, but this time, I couldn't. All I could do
was be with him.

BJ had a tremendous fear of needles, so every time he went for
tests, blood work, and scans, I went with him to talk him through
it. He wanted me there. He was given the diagnosis of renal cell

carcinoma stage three and was admitted into a private room within forty-eight hours. Five days later, he had an eight-hour surgery to remove a large mass, the size of a football, and his kidney. After the surgery, the surgeon told us the good news: all had gone well. The cancer hadn't spread to other parts of his body and the mass would be sent to be analyzed.

BJ had a follow-up appointment two weeks after surgery, and his doctor told him that everything looked good and his next check-up would be in six months. He told him that if cancer returns, it is usually within six months. Over the next couple of months, BJ recovered from surgery and looked much better. He resumed his normal life, ate well and regained some weight, and his morale was high. He had a completely new perspective on life. He enjoyed time with family and friends, and treasured his time at his cottage.

But during the Canada Day weekend, I received a phone call from my daughter who was with him at the cottage saying that BJ wasn't eating again and didn't look good. So on the Tuesday, I took him back to the hospital. The doctor told us that he was probably dehydrated and had overdone activities at the cottage, but to be safe, he scheduled some tests for him.

The worst day of my life was 12 August when we went to see the surgeon for test results. BJ looked worried, and I think he knew something was wrong. That day he received the diagnosis of terminal cancer, as it had spread into other organs. He looked at the doctor in disbelief and with fear, and he said, "There has to be something that could be done." The doctor replied that his cancer was very aggressive, too far spread, and all that could be done was to make him as comfortable as possible for at most two years. BJ turned to me and said, "Mom, my kids," and those words are engrained in my heart. As we left the office, BJ gave the doctor a hug and thanked him for giving him the past six months, and said he would make four years. As we walked down the hall, he took my hand said to me "I guess I'm going to see nanny before you do." BJ was then referred to an oncology team and was put on a chemo drug to prolong his life a little and to give him a better quality of life.

BJ was able to take his son Christian to the bus stop for his first days of school. You could see the weight of the world on his shoulders as he sat with his son. I couldn't imagine all the thoughts going through his head or what he was thinking. He withdrew a bit and needed to spend some alone time so he would go upstairs to his room, lie down, and watch television.

His one wish was to take his kids to Disney world, but his oncologist advised against leaving the country. We discussed this as a family and decided we would do it anyway and we would find a way to get us back if we had to. So we all went as a family, including his sister Natalie and niece Lilly. We rented BJ a scooter, as he was tiring easily. His legs continued swelling and retaining fluid. We were told to watch for clots, which were a sign of cancer progression.

Between August and November, BJ had to go back into the hospital once for a week, as he wasn't feeling well. During this visit, we completed forms for his wishes for when his condition would progress. This was difficult, but he did not want to be kept alive by machines—do not resuscitate. During those months, we had to bring him to our home a couple of times for a few days when his kids got sick, as his immune system was low. During these stays, I spent some amazing times with my son. We laughed and we cried and we hugged. These days were a special gift from my son.

We celebrated his thirty-second birthday by renting a meeting room at a hotel at the end of October. Until that point, BJ hadn't wanted to see anyone, but now he was ready. He cried when he left the banquet room at the end of the evening as did many of those who attended as he knew this was the last time he would see most of those folks and that this was his final goodbye to them. On Halloween, BJ went trick-or-treating with his wife, kids, sister Natalie, and niece Lilly. He was dressed as a sick patient in a wheelchair, and Natalie and Lori went out as doctors. On 5 November, we celebrated his daughter Chloe's second birthday. He was bloated but in good spirits, laughing, and eating well.

On 15 November, we were in his living room talking about how we would all spend Christmas. BJ wanted to have Christmas at his home with all the family. After an hour or so, he experienced a severe pain in his leg, so he went up to his room to lie down. That was the last time he saw his children and his home. He was taken to the hospital by ambulance, and he never came home again.

I stayed with him in the evening and overnight, and Lori came during the day after the kids went to school and daycare. The last day he was fully conscious was 17 November. He got weaker and groggier. Two days later, he had a nosebleed, and a specialist was called to cauterize the bleed, as it couldn't be stopped. She pulled a clot from his throat, which caused him to gag and bring up all the blood he had swallowed over numerous hours.

The next day, 20 November, BJ had a scan, and during it, he said to Lori, "I'm done." The scan showed that his body was full of clots. The doctor came to see us and told us there was nothing left to do except keep him comfortable and make this as easy as possible for him. Late that afternoon, I was beside him, and he grabbed my hand. In a strange way, I think he was trying to tell me his body was shutting down and that he was going. I just kept talking to him and comforting him. We told him how much we loved him and we held him. I told him to go find nanny and that she was waiting for him to show him the way. BJ passed away on Thursday 20 November at 5:55 p.m. We were all there with him. My son was gone! I felt numb. It was over. I now understand what people mean when they say a "hole in my heart." Life will never be the same for me because part of me is missing—the son I gave birth to, loved, and nourished for thirty-two years.

His funeral was a moving tribute to an amazing young man who gave so much to everyone who knew him. There was music and a photo presentation; his personal items were displayed around the room. I gave a eulogy, although I don't know how I got through it. It was like an out of body experience. I knew he was helping me; he was with me and was proud of me.

As BJ had requested during our talks, people donated money instead of flowers as BJ wanted us to purchase fold out chair beds for 5 East (cancer wing) at the Ottawa Hospital for families staying with their loved ones fighting cancer. We hold a "Bowling for BJ" event now every year on the anniversary of his death and continue to raise funds for these chair beds in his memory. It's a good way to spend a sad day with family, friends, and colleagues, which I'm sure he just loves!

BJ's biggest fear was leaving his cherished wife and children. I promised him two things: I would put a book together about his life so that his children would know who their daddy was when they got older, as they were only two and four and a half when he died; and I would volunteer when the time was right and sit with people dealing with cancer alone.

Since his passing, I have done everything I could to help with my grief so I can be there for his children—so that BJ can see them through my eyes. Although I am grateful to have them, as they are part of my son, there is still great sadness as I feel their dad should be here for them and not me. My family doctor has provided me with counselling, and I have also seen a private counsellor. I have taken part in a loss of child group at Bereaved Families of Ottawa, and I have read many books on grief, on the loss of child, and on the afterlife. I believe we will be together again.

I was raised Catholic but go to church only a few times a year. I speak directly to God and do the best I can to be a good person. My belief in an afterlife has been strengthened since my husband and I have received many signs from BJ since his passing. Some of these are:

I had my mom's funeral card under his pillow when he passed away, and I kept telling him to go and take her hand. I found this card in his bed at home a few days later when I was making their bed.

One night, I asked him for a sign—to send me a cardinal. The next morning, there was one on the hedge at home.

Two months after he died, the clock in my home stopped for no reason at 5:55 p.m. We took the battery out and put it back in, and it was fine.

One night when I was out staying with the grandchildren at their home, my husband woke up to the clocks in the house playing music that was played at BJ's funeral.

I often see cardinals and butterflies around me now and I find feathers and coins.

And so many more sign that are too numerous to mention and I continue to get them!

I don't understand why BJ was taken from us so young when there are so many bad people on earth. Maybe he was taken to guide the way for us. I will have to wait until the day he greets me to find out.

I miss him every day, and I talk to him every day. I often shed tears, and my heart will always have a hole in it. My life is different now that I cannot speak to him, touch him, hear him, hug him, or kiss him. I will never get over the loss of my child, but I get through every day and I manage, though differently, and with his help.

To my husband Barrie, who is my support and allows me to grieve freely, thank you. To my daughter Natalie and her daughter, Lilly, I love you so much and you mean the world to me. To my daughter-in-law Lori, you will always have a special place in my life. Thank you for loving my son the way you do. To my grandchildren Christian and Chloe, I love you just like your daddy does. To Pam and Paul, thank you for loving BJ like a son. To my brother-in-law Leo, thank you for being there to encourage BJ. To my sister Lynda, thank you for being my crutch! To my sisters Diane and Danielle and my brother Raymond, I love you both and thanks for understanding my pain. To BJ's friends and colleagues, you were all a huge part of his life and continue to be through me. You are all my reason for being where I am today. I couldn't get through this loss without you.

Forever in my heart, BJ. Love Mom, xxx.

# 21.
# Still

LINDA TURNER

TWENTY-SIX YEARS AGO TODAY, I was pregnant for the second time and within days of my due date. Twenty-six years ago tomorrow, I would arrive at the doctor's office and be told they could not find a heartbeat. My daughter 's death and birth—"in utero" as one sympathy card referred to it—would provide me with life lessons I wasn't seeking but that I can now say are valuable and even cherished. It gives me solace and a warm connection to write about my daughter Rosa and how she influenced my life and the life of those around her. It was even more remarkable, as my mother aptly noted, since she didn't even take one breath.

All I have of Rosa is a lock of hair and inked footprints on paper. My other three babies never had their footprints inked, but I am grateful the nurses went ahead and performed this special ritual. It was a powerfully symbolic opportunity to launch me into my grieving process, shepherding me to the first of what author and counsellor Alan Wolfelt calls the "mourner's six needs of reconcil-iation." I suppose I required a double dose of the "acknowledge the reality of the death" need. Yes, my daughter died, and yes, she was really born. Without those tiny footprints, I could have too easily snuggled into a denial den—my grief as hard and solid as marble—and pretended I was not the mother of a baby who died.

On 21 August 1991, I walked out of the Georges Dumont hos-pital in Moncton, New Brunswick, after being told there was no heartbeat, as I told them I needed to move my car. By the time I reentered, the obstetrician had launched a hunt for me—irritated the nurses had permitted me to be alone after receiving such devastating news. I recall hearing the doctor in an adjoining room phoning the regional children's hospital. He stumbled in English, his second language, as he awkwardly blurted he needed to have an autopsy because he had delivered a baby who was *mort-né*: "She was born dead." Using "stillborn" instead might have swept around the edges of the reality I needed to acknowledge, over and over, until I had no choice but to believe it.

Many aspects of the experience have been vitally important to me. I love the nurse who spoke frankly with composure and deep compassion: "Linda, you saw the screen. You need to know that this happens, and there is absolutely nothing you did that could have caused it." I needed her honesty and assurance.

I do not understand why after delivery when I was first offered the chance to see and hold Rosa that I refused. Perhaps I was not yet on board with wanting to acknowledge the death, but I recall a mental reaction I had that touching any dead body, but especially a baby's, was morbid. The nurses persisted until I could see they were struggling to have me see this newborn lying lifeless in the *pouponnière*. I relented then and have been forever grateful I was coaxed to hold my daughter in my arms. I had already given permission for them to take a photo that would be on file if ever in the future I might want it. The next day I asked for it.

Friends and family helped me acknowledge the reality of Rosa's death, with every card, every hospital visit, every tear, and every embrace. Alan Wolfelt does not expect even the heartiest of grievers to be relentless in meeting the first need, as they may have to push away the reality of death to survive. The reality slapped me in the face sometimes, and other times was a dark and drenched cloak that descended.

My partner, Louis—a very practical man described by friends as salt of the earth—had to pick up the tiny white wooden box with my daughter's body inside from the hospital morgue. He drove our daughter to our home village to find the priest for her burial. But first he drove to the public health office to deliver the death certificate and complete the paperwork. "Did he realize that he was required by law to have her buried?" a clerk asked him. I have often wondered what else he thought Louis might have had in mind. To take her home and put her in the freezer?

Finally, relieved to be driving back to familiar countryside on that hot August day, Louis unfortunately discovered that, in 1991 at least, local village priests actually took a day off. With no other choice—and I told you he is practical—he brought Rosa home and kept the bigger-than-a-bread-box white wooden cradle alternative in the only cool storage unit we had, the freezer, until the next day when I was released from hospital and the priest was back at work. I have continuously been thankful that our dear daughter came home and that she, her big sister Stephanie, papa, and *maman* travelled the ten miles to the cemetery together. As we were passing her grandparents' home, Grandmother **Mémère** and little cousin Rébeka, wildflower bouquets in hand, were at the roadside flagging us down. In an inappropriately festive spirit, Louis's mother responded to my tears by expressing her firm belief that "you have an angel looking out for you now."

## EMBRACING PAIN

Wolfelt says the second need mourners have is to embrace the pain. What did it mean in my case to embrace the pain? For the first twenty-four hours, the medication I was urged to take did not allow me to feel anything but detachment and intrigue that my irises could grow so large. I can still hear myself on the phone calling people close to me and reporting in a matter of fact voice these things happen and they needn't worry about me. I firmly declined more medication after that day.

During those few days in hospital, I appeared completely together, handling it well to nurses and visitors who observed me. But the instant they left and I was alone, emotion would spill out and through me. Back at home, my pattern was to privately let loose and to let myself respond as my natural impulses dictated—stunned, immobile, angry. I cried and often the sobs that came out would be at the tip of a period when others saw me as doing well. Occasionally, the dam broke even in others' presence. On a camping trip a few weeks after Rosa's death and throughout the spectacular autumn beauty in the Gaspé region, I found myself in a mode of cherishing life, cherishing Stephanie, and cherishing Louis. The balance was maintained until we pulled into a gas station and a well-meaning acquaintance recognized us, approached our vehicle, and popped the question "so, where's the baby?" In one second, I was reduced to a sobbing heap. It was an honest and natural question, and my reaction, in turn, was honest. I was having a "grief burst"— an "out of the blue" heavy downpour.

More often, I kept the pain under wraps except when coming within eyesight of my closest friends, who could see through to my pain and wouldn't let me pretend, ignore, or avoid. Early on, I would break down in sobs in front of them—sobs that had been politely and valiantly withheld from public consumption. Even when I tried to push my "these things happen" mantra, my closest friend insisted "maybe these things happen, but I wish that Rosa was here and that she wasn't one of the ones who died."

By embracing my pain, there were moments when I gave in to it. I let myself feel it so deeply that it shuddered through me. Similar to what I believe it would feel like to fall over a huge embankment and know there was no turning around, I surrendered to the pain of loss and sadness. My dearest friends opened space for me to say what I dared not admit in casual company—I tortured myself thinking that something I had done must have caused her to become motionless. Part of embracing the pain for me was daring to explore and name the aspects of the death that I didn't understand, couldn't accept, and was tortured by. More than anything, I needed friends to simply listen as I sifted through hypotheses, although I admit that when my childhood friend Margie quipped "the only thing you are guilty of Linda is stupidity for thinking you did something to cause her death," I found the message, delivered in her typically sarcastic and humorous style, to be welcome medicine.

A father whose twelve-year-old daughter died during an asthma attack and who had lost two other of his children to stillbirth used to travel with me to support group meetings. We chatted about all kinds of things on the way there and on the way back. But during the meeting, in the safe and comforting circle of other parents who knew the heartache of death of their cherished offspring, I would cry and sob and release my anguish. That is how I embraced the pain.

## REMEMBERING ROSA

The third need Wolfelt highlights is to remember the person who died. Well-wishers wanting to be helpful sometimes encourage us to move on by saying "you can't bring them back" or rush us into the "have another baby stage," when what we need is to keep— perhaps even create—a memory associated with our deceased child.

The first Christmas after her death, I stitched something in her honour: a bright yellow felt sun with a smiling face that was the topping for our tree for many years after. I spent the Christmas full moon weekend at a local Trappistine monastery to have time with her memory alone—engaged in readings and writing, I felt closer to her.

How does one remember someone who was only known through gentle kicks in the abdomen scarcely noticed because a toddler was taking central stage? I go back to discovering I was pregnant and to photographs of me pregnant with an "I'm due in August" button. I appreciate the many gifts we received, such as the hand-crocheted blanket I still have, to welcome her.

I remember us at the cemetery—a small and informal gathering, the priest in blue jeans and a white smock top, which fit our style far more comfortably than a church would have. Many years later, when our three other children were adolescents, it felt like the right day to offer them the chance to look at Rosa's photo if they wished. Stephanie couldn't bring herself to do so; the other two were curious and did. There is beauty despite the waxy skin and deep crimson lips. Holding the photo provides a hint of remembrance and a heavyweight connection. My precious ring, worn daily, holds a stone for all four children, as does my favourite pendant.

When Stephanie was a young schoolchild, her teacher instructed her to draw her family, and she insisted on including her sister Rosa. I am grateful she had an understanding teacher who listened to Stephanie, even though the teacher had not been told about Rosa. Recently, Sébastien, now twenty-one and studying physiotherapy at Laval University, took a course in obstetrics. I loved talking to him about whether my being Rh positive could have been a factor in her death. I will continue to feel the need to create avenues, trails, and paths that root Rosa in our memory.

Babies and children are buried together in our local cemetery, which gives the area a parklike atmosphere. I have noticed many headstones reach back to the forties, the fifties, the sixties, and the seventies. I learn through them that a neighbour or a teacher or a local business owner also knew and survived the inexplicable pain of losing an infant or young child.

## WHO AM I NOW? A NEW SELF-IDENTITY IS BORN

Alan Wolfelt believes that when we find ourselves dealing with the death of a loved one, developing a new self-identity is necessary.

The day the doctor who delivered Rosa phoned me at work about eight months later to say the autopsy revealed nothing about why she died was a particularly difficult one. I'd been holding my breath waiting for the call. I was expecting to have an explanation to replace the ones that surfaced regularly. Had I eaten something bacteria ridden? Was it because I mowed the lawn and accidentally inhaled gas fumes?

His apologetic summary was devastating. If I would never know the cause of death, how could I move forward? Being clear about the cause might have led me to become someone who fought and advocated for the bigger cause. But there continued to be no cause to fight for.

In the interim between Rosa's death and getting the news, I applied to a PhD program. The anonymous peer review committee examining my grant application must have been scratching their heads trying to understand how I'd come up with the topic of researching and developing supports for women dealing with guilt for behaviour associated with infant death. Writing has so often enabled me to move past debilitating emotion, and in this case, a doctoral research grant application played a part as I tried to fill my cavernous void.

However, I wasn't accepted for that program, which was something I counted on so I could say, "there, that explains why she had to die... I was meant to do this PhD program, and if I had two little ones underfoot it wouldn't have been possible." I now had to search deeper to find out who I would become, if not the mother of two daughters close in age or a doctoral student.

Who I became was a person who learned beauty, solace, and shimmering humanity exist in reaching out for support and offering support. Because of my experience, I have become a person who wants to be available to listen to others who have walked a similar path and to share with them. Living through a scenario that wasn't supposed to happen, I have realized that even though I can't control what may happen or that I won't see my infant develop into a child and grow, enough strength can still be found within me to get through.

## WHAT'S IT ALL ABOUT?
## THE ONGOING SEARCH FOR MEANING

I was a relative newcomer *"anglaise"* living in a very Acadian community. Not a Catholic and unknown to the village priest, I appreciated that he didn't propose rituals or prayers. I commented, "no doubt one day I will be able to see why this had to happen"— implying that some good should come from all despair. I assumed he would say something about God's plan unfolding, but his comment "or perhaps you'll never understand why" caught me off-guard. His statement hinted at a needed notion: answers cannot always be found, but this, too, is life and acceptance is vital.

## DON'T GO IT ALONE:
## RECEIVING ONGOING SUPPORT FROM OTHERS

I am typically a person who jumps at the chance to meet new people and to attend community activities. I am definitely a joiner. But exposing myself as someone needing to ask others for support or understanding is a different story. Initially, I even pushed my husband away.

I resisted recommendations to join the newly formed support group for parents whose child had died. It took a coincidence, which looked suspiciously like divine intervention, to make me take my guard down. On a day when I was in my solitary depths of despair, silently praying to be released from the pain and inertia, the telephone rang. It was Darlene, the woman who had started the Miramichi group, Sunrise, after the death of her twin newborns.

She introduced herself, and I said "Oh you were probably asked to call about the support group." She seemed confused. "No, I was calling to remind you that tomorrow is Stephanie's immunization appointment," she said. As a nurse, she didn't usually make the reminder calls, but that day she asked the administrative assistant if there was anything she could do to help her out, and she'd been given my name to call. I decided I should attend the meeting.

Today, twenty-six years since Rosa Anne Marie Turner-Chiasson came into my life, her papa and I went to the Rogersville cemetery. We had recently put fresh white paint on the wooden cross her grandfather made to mark her burial ground. Today, we added a stone on which her name is beautifully engraved with a small Celtic emblem meaning everlasting love. Saturated in love, we drove home.

The light was flashing on the telephone when we returned home—a voicemail message from Rosa's younger sister Geneviève calling from Colorado during a trek across the U.S. This was eerily odd because in the past five years of living in Australia and the UK, and travelling through nearly fifty countries, Geneviève never once called home from overseas. She said in her voice message "I don't know why I'm calling." She had dialed the home number at exactly the moment when we were at the cemetery placing the stone on Rosa's grave.

No one in the family needs convincing that Mémère had been right, twenty-six years ago, when she said we would have an angel looking out for us. I believe it was Rosa who whispered to her little sister, "Gen, you should call home; this is a special family day."

# 22.
# Living My Best Life for My Son, Chris

ELAINE DEAN

CHRISTOPHER IS MY FIRST CHILD. He was born on 10 December 1993. I never really imagined being a mum, but once I knew I would be, I was over the moon. With great enthusiasm, I learned everything I could about being pregnant and was thrilled beyond belief when Chris finally arrived, albeit a bit late. His birth was difficult, lasting more than twenty-four hours.

Afterward, when everyone else went away, we both lay on the bed together for hours just looking into each other's eyes. I marvelled at this beautiful baby in front of me and will always remember his blue eyes and the precious time we spent together. I have had many occasions since then to look into those eyes and wish he were physically here right in front of me so I could do so again.

Right from the very beginning, I always wanted to be with Chris. I created my own song about how much I loved him and how wonderful he was. I sang it to him as I rocked him to sleep. I still feel this way about him, as I do about his younger brother Julian and my husband Sean, who has been part of our lives since 2000. As Chris grew older, I imagined there was an invisible elastic band between us, which just kept getting longer as he grew more independent. But it has always been there. I imagine it is still there now, only longer still.

We had been through some trying times together, Christopher, Julian, and I. When Chris was five, I was diagnosed with breast cancer. When I was wheeled into the operating room for my surgery, I showed a picture of Christopher and Julian to my surgical team; I asked them to make sure I made it through for my children. I was off work for a year afterward, during which time I focussed my energy on getting better for them. I used to think about my recovery as having a beginning, a middle, and an end, which I had hoped would have a positive outcome. I had always believed that if you worked hard and applied yourself you would achieve your dreams. Not all at once, but over time, through incremental steps, with effort and discipline and some good luck on your side now and then.

Before Christopher started school, we spent time painting the characters of the *Land before Time* on our back fence. Together with his brother, we played and danced to music in the backyard, in the kitchen, and in the living room; we went for daily walks along the canal, and we spent many hours drawing at our kitchen table. We had a chalkboard, and I spent many evenings after they had gone to bed drawing new pictures for them, which delighted them in the mornings when they got up. We spent our summer days together at Lac Lapeche, playing in the sand and in the water. We both decided that when we grew up we would be angels because then we would have the opportunity to help other people.

We enrolled together in tae kwon do at the Canterbury Community Centre, and this became an important part of his life. One day when he was in grade eight, Chris was sitting on the bench on our front porch when I came home from work. As soon as he saw me, he broke out in tears. He had been in a fight at school and had a black eye. I held him close, and after a while, he felt better. Years later, he ended up achieving his second dan black belt, and started teaching taekwondo to others. Math and science always came easy to Chris, so it was no surprise he chose to study architecture. As part of his application, he put together an art portfolio. I helped him assemble it at our dining table, and his talent brought me to tears. So many pieces, all beautifully executed. I still have many pieces of Chris's art.

When we went together to the open house at the University of Waterloo's School of Architecture, he was thrilled. I knew he would thrive there. We found him a place to live with three other students in a house close to the university.

It was hard to let him go. But I knew in my heart that it was the right decision for Chris. When he headed off to university, he was so happy. He enjoyed university and socializing with friends. His friends have shared their stories with me about him, about how he would show up and make them feel better when they were stressed—how they felt better because he was there with them.

In February 2013, Chris posted a favourite message of mine on Facebook. It captures who he is and makes me smile: "sometimes, i wonder 'why am i torturing myself going to architecture school?' but then, i remember—i am destined. Destined to be great. I am starchitect material. so all ma friends, I'll design you a *haus* one day (that's german for house in case you didn't know). And it will be dope. msg me!"

On 21 December 2013, the day before Christopher was supposed to come home for Christmas holidays, tragedy struck. I had spoken to him just two days before, after he finished his final exam. I remember what he said: "Hi Mum. I still have a workshop to finish. I'm working hard. But I'm out right now having dinner with my friends. Gotta go. I love you Mum."

He had asked me previously if I would pick him up and drive him home, and then he ended up arranging a ride back to Ottawa with a friend. The day before he was to come home, I made his favourite dishes in anticipation for his arrival. I still wish to this day that I had driven there to pick him up myself.

That night, we had friends over for dinner. Julian was already home from university for the holiday. When we heard the phone ring, Julian answered it, and then handed me the phone. His dad told me that Chris had been hit by a car and was on his way by ambulance to Hamilton. We went to the airport right away and caught a flight to Toronto. I cried all the way there, while Sean and Julian held my hands. Then we rented a car and drove to Hamilton General Hospital. It was during an ice storm, and driving was dangerous. We went to the emergency unit, and the sympathetic look of the attendant we spoke to registered. We didn't get to see Chris right away because he was in the operating room. His surgeon removed part of his skull to allow his brain to swell. He then came to the waiting room to speak with us, and said that if Chris were an older person, he would not survive. Because he was so young, he had a chance. We knew it was grim, but I lived in hope for my Christopher.

How could this have happened? Some friends were having dinner together at Chris's house before they headed off for the holidays. They were looking forward to their first co-op placement in January but weren't sure yet which cities they would be in. Chris was hoping to go to New York. He headed out on foot to pick up a bottle of wine. It was dark, just before 6:00 p.m., when a car turned into the intersection he was crossing and hit him. When he didn't come back, his friends realized something was wrong. They searched for him and eventually found out he had been taken to the hospital.

I will never forget walking into his hospital room and seeing Chris lying there. Up until then, I had hoped they had it wrong and that this was happening to someone else. My beautiful boy still looked beautiful, with no marks on him, but he was unconscious.

We spent the next two weeks at the hospital, and met regularly with his surgical team. It was Christmas time, which meant that the full complement of staff wasn't there. There was Christmas music playing in the small cafeteria, which was still open. To this day, I still can't tolerate Christmas music. Every Thursday, a new neurosurgeon was assigned to Chris's case. His nurses changed every two to three days. There was no multidisciplinary team to support. Chris was put on a machine to lower his body temperature in the hope of reducing his brain swelling. He had multiple brain contusions and had five brain scans to assess his condition. His doctors seemed to know what was going to happen but were helpless just as we were.

All I could do was be there for Chris. On one of those occasions, I was holding his hand and praying. He squeezed my hand several times. And I squeezed back. That was early on, but after that, nothing. His doctors tried to wake him, to no avail. Then he had a massive stroke. We were taken into a room with his surgical team, where they delivered the blow: there was no hope he would recover. They showed us the scan. I asked them to do another one to be sure and just in case a miracle could happen. There was no miracle, and they knew for sure. It was hard to believe this really was happening.

Then we were faced with having to take Chris off life support. We knew he would want to donate his organs. His last few days on this earth, I spent with him. I slept in his bed, held him, and sang to him—the very same song I sang to him when he was a baby. His friends from high school came and spent time with him. I was there with him the moment he died, the morning of 7 January 2014. His blood pressure dropped. I felt something happening, a surge, and then I saw his light move away from his body. His lips turned white. I screamed and cried for I don't know how long. It seemed like time stood still. Afterward, the chaplain and Chris's neurosurgeon came in to talk with me. Sean was by my side.

For a long time afterward, I relived every minute of the time I spent in hospital with Chris. And I relived every decision I made, which might have resulted in a different outcome. What if I had phoned him earlier that day, which could have changed what happened next? I also heard many stories about Chris from his friends, who rallied around and helped me through this difficult time, along with my own friends and family. My world was truly shaken and was turned upside down.

When Chris was in hospital, I met his new girlfriend Kate for the first time on her birthday. After Chris passed away, we held a celebration of life for him in Ottawa. At his service, Kate said, "Not only did Chris make me incredibly happy, he also made me feel safe, appreciated, and beautiful." His professor Terri said: "Chris was always smiling. Some people 'just smile,' but with Chris, his entire body seemed to be part of the smile." His tae kwon do teacher spoke from his heart. We all wore our coolest t-shirts and shared our stories of Chris.

The pain has been at the brink of unbearable. When it first happened, every time I saw someone his age, I asked myself why my Chris? I wanted so much to see him walk up our path and come in our front door to give me just one more of his big bear hugs and to see his wonderful face—talk with him and hear his voice. Every time I saw a young man riding a bike or just walking across the street, I wanted so much for it to be Chris. I looked at the clouds in the sky in hope he would draw pictures for me. I played his music in the car and imagined he was sitting beside me. I wore his clothes. I created photo albums of him and of the photos he took. I hung his art on our walls. I wanted to know everything about Chris. And yes, I cried every single day. For more than a year. In the second year, I cried most days.

I often listen to Chris's voice mail message Sean recorded for me. I talk to Chris, and I believe he is still here with us, just in a different form. I know that my belief is a choice, and I choose to believe it. I also know we will be together again one day in the future. I imagine that Chris visits his friends and me, and he still looks out for us.

Chris grew up to be a smart, loving, talented, and happy young man. His life was too short. I wish he had been here longer, and I know he would have realized all of his dreams if had had more time. My hope for Chris is that he is now the angel we both said we wanted to be when he was small.

The promise I made to Chris before he died is that I will live my best life for him. This, it turns out, is not all that easy. Before I lost Chris, I simply didn't know grieving could last a lifetime. Now I know this with certainty. There seems to be consensus that the second year is the worst. The numbness has worn off; you have to accept it really is true. Yet you are still here, figuring out how to go forward with a hole in your heart. This is where I am still. Sometimes, I catch myself saying "Chris, please come home." It is still hard for me to accept there is nothing I can do to change this outcome.

The intensity of my grief has lessened, and time is no longer just melting away. I still cry. I will always miss my Chris. My life has become more about just taking things one step at a time. And if that doesn't work, then a different step in another direction. I have good days and bad days. But the good days are gradually becoming more frequent. Sean and I still see the other parents in our support group, who have become good friends. I see my life differently now. I strive to do my best by focussing more on the people important to me. Sean and I have decided we will always celebrate Chris's birthday because we are so glad he was born. We light candles for him at the dinner table. December and January will always be difficult months of the year for me to get through.

There are now two trees planted in Chris's memory: one at Canterbury High School and the other in Cambridge at the School of Architecture. One first-year architecture student now receives the annual Christopher Dean Moran award. Chris received his degree posthumously in 2017. I was honoured to be there to accept

Chris's degree on his behalf, even though it was difficult to hear all the speeches about looking forward to new beginnings. I was invited to speak after the ceremony, and I thanked Chris's friends for remembering him. They keep Chris close in their hearts. For me, they are more than a class of graduates, they are a caring community of Chris's friends—now my friends too—who keep his memories alive.

As his mum, I will always hold him close in my heart and in my thoughts, just as I have from the very beginning. My love for Chris will last my lifetime. I have so many precious memories of him. Even though I can't look into his beautiful blue eyes any more, I see them in my mind's eye. I hear his voice and his laughter, and see his smile and his silly grin. Both my unconditional love for him and the pain of losing him will always be there. He is part of me and always will be.

# 23.
# Goodnight Irene

SUSAN DOYLE LAWRENCE

*Life can only be understood backwards, but it must be lived forwards.*
—Kierkegaard

IT ALL BEGAN AT OUR February Compassionate Friends meeting when we each spoke about memories of our child's birth day or birthday. For some of us, this brought back positive memories. Yes, those times were gone now, and no, they would not return, but they did happen. For some parents, though, thoughts associated with their child's special date brought mostly feelings of sorrow.

My thoughts could easily have turned to judgment: "What is wrong with them that they cling to the negative instead of focusing on the positive?" (Goodness, don't we hear that one often enough out there?) My attitude could have been one of pity: "Poor things; what a shame. Their child did not live long enough, was not celebrated enough while alive, and now the parents are suffering. How sad. They need help." (Don't we all just love to be helped by people with this attitude?) Instead, this being a TCF sharing meeting, my heart immediately went to a place of compassion—some of their reactions I could understand already; others I sought to understand.

We talked about triggers—otherwise known as grief hooks or grief landmines or bombs. You know what I mean. You are cleaning out a kitchen drawer and you come across some tiny reminder of your child, misfiled by place and by time. Your defenses are down; you are totally vulnerable. You are pierced by the intensity of your emotional reaction.

But I left the meeting feeling we had not really come up with an answer to the real question: triggers can happen to any of us at any time, so what do we do when we trip over one of these grief landmines? I do not want to remain so exposed and vulnerable to unexpected pain.

## TURNING POINT 1998

I can tell you where I was standing as well as the colour of the cloth in my hand. I can tell you what the weather was like outside and what it was like inside. All these things I knew on Sunday 6 September 1998.

Our thirty-one-year-old daughter, Irene, had died just before midnight on Thursday 3 September. Her funeral was planned for Tuesday 8 September. We were in that suspended state following a sudden tragedy; we were caught between what seemed both impossible and incomprehensible—our stark reality. As I stood at the kitchen counter, wiping the same spot for the twelfth time, I said to my husband, "I don't know how we are going to get through this, but I know that we will."

Later, in the middle of the night, I got up and went out into the garden. The ground beneath me still held the warmth of August, but the air about me was crisp with the reality of autumn approaching. I stood on the back lawn and looked up at the clear black sky. The tops of the surrounding trees formed a dark circle around clusters of stars overhead. And as I gazed up at those stars, they seemed to become apertures, openings in the black canopy above, with rays streaming through—rays not just of light but also of understanding and knowledge from somewhere in the great beyond. In that moment of transcendence I knew, I absolutely knew, that Irene was at peace. Yes, the name Irene means "peace," I reminded myself. Now, we just have to find our own peace here on earth.

That peace was to prove elusive. In the days, weeks, and months ahead, my husband fell ever deeper into depression. Eventually, he was diagnosed with posttraumatic stress disorder. Irene's young son, Michael, fared no better. From the moment he was told of his mother's death, he went into deep denial. We've been through years of treatments and interventions, years of trials and hardships with him. I don't think it will ever be over.

But my marriage is. We did start out on the grief journey together, and tried to provide mutual support. Our main focus, though, was on young Michael. Irene had been a single parent, and she had made legal provisions for us to become her son's legal guardians "if anything should happen." When the worst did happen, Michael was seven and starting grade two. Overnight, we became fulltime parents of a troubled young boy.

My husband and I have different parenting styles. When our own children were growing up, he worked in remote logging camps and was away for weeks, sometimes months at a time, so I was, in effect, a single parent. There was no "let me talk this over with your dad," or "wait till your father gets home." I had to make the decisions and stand by them. This practice held me in good stead as my role suddenly changed from grandparent to parent. Young Michael learned that Granny could always be relied on to be there and to dish the straight goods. No fooling around. No caving in. Papa, on the other hand, was a softie. He would say, "No, no, no, well OK." He would also kid around and make up fanciful stories— stories that had reality at the core, but with, well ... let's call them embellishments. Michael learned to ask, "Granny, is that true?"

I've said that Michael went into denial at the time of his mother's death. This worked when he was awake, but at night, he could not keep the demons at bay. He would wake from nightmares and crawl in with us in the master bedroom. One of us would comfort him until he went back to sleep; then, we would tuck him back into his own bed. But we both needed our sleep, so I started sleeping in the spare bedroom, and we would take turns either getting Michael or getting sleep. For the first few months, we were able to continue with marital intimacy, but as time passed, the wanting and the willingness faded away. For my husband, they were replaced by long periods of emotional withdrawal, alternating with flashes of anger. Respect waned. Then the love was gone. We have been informally separated ever since.

On that Sunday morning in September 1998, I was standing at my kitchen counter, tidying, cleaning, wiping, as though putting my house in order would put my life back into order. It was a clear, bright day outside. All was turmoil inside. All these things I knew that day. What I did not know was that when I said we would get through this, I could only speak for myself. I did not know my marriage would not survive. As for the cloth, it was a faded pink facecloth. It had been a wedding gift. I have it yet.

## GOODNIGHT, IRENE

"Come quick! Irene's stopped breathing!" Those words would forever change my life and the lives of those I love. The call came around 11:00 p.m. on Thursday 3 September 1998. At the end of a long day, late in a busy week, I had gone to bed after ten, only to be disturbed by a call on my business phone shortly after. I headed back to bed. When the household phone rang soon after that, I decided to let the answering machine take the call. I could deal with the matter in the morning. But when the phone rang again immediately, I thought I had better answer it. It was James, our daughter Irene's partner. "Come quick! Irene's stopped breathing! The ambulance is here!"

"We'll be right there." I dashed downstairs where my husband had dozed off in his chair. "Mike, wake up! Irene's stopped breathing. Get in the car. I'll drive." I threw on some clothes, grabbed my purse, keys, and a cell phone, and we headed from our home in the community of Langford, toward Victoria. Racing in on the Trans-Canada Highway, as we approached Victoria General Hospital, we called James, and he told us the ambulance had taken Irene to the Royal Jubilee Hospital, which was closer to their home, so we headed across town to "The Jub."

Amazingly, when we got there, the emergency ward was quiet, with no one waiting around except James's mom, who had rushed over while James remained at Irene's apartment to stay with Michael. "What happened?" we asked her. "How is she?"

Meanwhile, the nurses tried to herd us into an incredibly ugly, depressing little room down the hall. While we were driving to the hospital, of course, "the worst" had crossed our minds. But we still had the expectation that if you can get someone to medical attention immediately, they will be all right. Just dial 911, and you're guaranteed a good outcome. Sure, they might need stitches or a cast or time in the hospital, but they certainly wouldn't die. The daughter who had been bouncing around our home that very afternoon could not be in danger of dying a few hours later. We expected in a few minutes a nurse would come out and say, "You can go in and see your daughter now," the way they had the night little Michael was born. That night the news was, "It's a boy, a big healthy boy. Irene's doing fine." This night we expected something along the lines of "She's had a seizure, but she'll be fine."

Only she wasn't fine. She was already dead. When she had stopped breathing, James had called 911 and started CPR; the two ambulance crews had attempted to revive her. At the hospital, they tried everything they could to restart her heart. Nothing worked. After midnight, a haggard doctor came to the door of the ugly, depressing little room and told us she was dead. My husband let out a desperate cry and started tearing at the furniture. I just stood up, walked across to the door, and said to the doctor, "But doctor, we have already lost one child." (Our son Michael had died thirty years earlier from disappearance and drowning.) I then went out into the hall and started making calls to the family.

Thus began the most difficult year of our lives.

### CHRISTMAS WITH MUMMY

We were determined that Michael would have a merry Christmas. We had observed too many holidays that could not be celebrated joyfully because, years ago, a death had happened near that date. He was a little kid, and little kids needed to have a Christmas with lots of noise and excitement and visitors, and skating, baking, shopping, putting up lights, laughing, playing games, staying up past your bedtime, hiding the presents, singing carols, and eating turkey dinner. And yes, oh yes, the presents. Under the tree.

Only we didn't feel like celebrating. It was only three months since Irene had died, and we were still in shock, still deep in mourning. We dreaded Christmas without Irene, without her laughter. Oh, how we missed her. How could we have Christmas without Irene, without Mummy?

A Victoria Hospice Society notice in the newspaper gave me an idea: we could have two Christmases, one with Mummy and one without her. Our Christmas with Mummy would last a whole week, beginning with the hospice's Celebrate a Life ceremony on Saturday, when lights are lit on a tree as a tribute to loved ones who are no longer with us. The Hospice Service of Remembrance, the following Sunday, would be a fitting close to the week.

Our second Christmas, the "merry" one, would be more than a week later, so not only would the two be very different, they would be distinctly separate. We did go to the Celebrate a Life ceremony, but were disappointed that we did not get to individually light the white bulbs on the tree. Instead, the main speaker turned them all on at once. And little Michael was not interested in the adult speeches. He wasn't interested in being there at all, for that matter. As at the time of Irene's funeral, he chose not to actively participate; he just hung out around the edge of events. My husband and I pinned up ribbons in memory of loved ones who have died (oh, there are too many of them!), but Michael, true to form, chose not to do so.

During the following week, we put together albums of remembrance, one for each smaller family unit within our very large extended family. We included photos of Irene from babyhood to motherhood. We put in examples of her poetry, from the little girl, the teen, the young adult. We included written tributes others had sent us. Michael learned a lot about the person his mother was before she became his mummy.

The following Sunday we attended the hospice's Service of Remembrance, held in the University of Victoria's Interfaith Chapel where Irene had been married eight years earlier. We dressed in our Sunday best, and our family joined us there for the excellent service. We had readings and speeches, and lots of music and songs, even young people playing ukuleles. Michael was fidgety. This was too close to the action for him. We just reminded him of polite behaviour. Granny and Papa and the rest of the family wanted to participate, so he needed to support us by being patient. After the service, we visited the cemetery where Irene's cremated remains were to be interred. We showed Michael where our parents, uncles, and grandparents are buried, and then showed him where his mummy's place would be. We explained what would happen when we placed her ashes there at some time in the future, when we were ready.

From there, we went to the house of Irene's aunt to gather with the whole family for afternoon tea. We gave out our albums of remembrance, one to each family group. These would be our Christmas gifts this year, but they were far too emotionally charged to be wrapped in bright paper and placed under the tree. Thus, our week of Christmas with Mummy ended.

Was our other Christmas merry? No, not merry, but we did have moments of peace and joy, for which we are thankful. We had found our way through our first Christmas without Irene, without Mummy.

## MY FIRST CHILD

We all have different ways of finding meaning in the events of our lives. For me, making sense of things involves language, so when I heard about a grief workshop that involved writing poetry, I signed up right away. In one exercise, the writing prompt was "firsts," and my mind immediately went to thoughts of the birth of my first baby, Michael, and how his death by disappearance and drowning was my first experience with a significant loss.

**Firstborn Son**
**Michael Frank Lawrence 1965-1968**

Your birth was my first delivery.
Your wrinkled pink body was handed to me,
swaddled in a blue flannelette receiving blanket.
Gazing at your wee face, I wondered about your future.
There were red roses back in my room.

Three years later your body was handed to us again,
this time encased in a grey steel canister, welded shut.
"Don't open it," they said. "Don't look."
There were white roses on your casket.

Your death was my first delivery
from innocence.

Daughter Irene was our poet, our singer, our writer, our musician. I was none of those things until after she died, so whenever a poem comes to me now, I feel as though I should credit her as the author—which I suspect she truly is. I just hold the pen and write as she dictates.

## Blue Butterfly at Thetis Lake 24 May 2009

One brilliant blue butterfly
Reminds me of two beautiful blue eyes
And blue irises in your wedding bouquet.

And of one
Rustling blue taffeta graduation gown
Worn first at seventeen, in joy,
And worn one
Final, silent time
As you lay in your coffin.

Blue butterfly,
How can your fragile wings carry
Such heavy blue memories?

in memory of Irene Susan Lawrence,
5 May 1967 – 3 September 1998

# 24.
# Life after Losing My Son

INGRID DRAAYER

I**T HAS BEEN NINE YEARS** since I lost my twenty-seven-year-old first-born son in a tragic accident. Those years have changed me significantly, and they have changed the relationships I have with others, both family and friends. I am not the same person I once was: how could I be? I will never return to my old self; I have been forever changed. When something so final and so profound happens, when the world as you knew has turned upside down and ripped apart, you see the world and your place in it very, very differently.

After the initial overwhelming outpouring of condolences and support, and the cards (in the hundreds), the flowers, the gift baskets, and the casseroles, my partner and I were left pretty much alone ("we didn't want to bother you; we wanted to leave you in peace"). Apart from a few people who have remained constant in my life, most others have disappeared. Those I thought would always be there for me are not, and, surprisingly, some of those I barely knew have become supporters and true friends. I was left grieving my son, but did not expect to be grieving the loss of friends and family.

Those of us who have lost children might see ourselves living in a parallel universe among whole nuclear families. It takes courage to navigate the social minefield, to put on your game face, suck up your grief, carry on, and interact with the people in your community and at your workplace. Coping day to day requires more energy than you might realize—getting out there, doing groceries, going about life—where you are going to inevitably run into people from your "former" life. What ensues is often an awkward and usually brief conversation. Even being asked how you are becomes a loaded question, and most people do not want to hear an honest answer.

The true gifts are the friends I now have—new ones who know me only as the person I am now, and old friends who have stuck by me and with whom I have developed deeper and more meaningful relationships. I do not have the energy to engage in shallow or conditional friendships, and the effort required for small talk drains me. One important group of new friends is other mothers who have lost children. We meet socially; we go out for dinner. We laugh, and we cry, but best of all, we can just be ourselves, our new selves.

I have watched myself, rather out-of-body, feeling so different from who I thought I was, so changed, and reflecting on who I am now. I believe my "after" self to be better in many ways than my "before" self. I live my life much more simply, stripped down to the essentials. Material things are the least important, true solid relationships the most important. I live my life honouring my son by trying to be a good person and concentrating on the things that bring me pleasure and peace, like gardening and cooking for the people I love. I am not too busy to pause to watch the fleeting beauty of a butterfly or a sudden stunning rainbow.

I live mostly in the moment, quite deliberately so, as I cannot think about the past; it is much too painful. The future for me has been altered, since it no longer includes my son. I try not to look at photographs of our family before. When I do, I see faces, captured in another time, all of us so innocent, unaware of the horror and the pain that would descend upon us. My oldest son, with his big radiant smile, his life would be cut so short; his younger sister and brother who had never known life without him, unaware they would one day become (surreally) older than their brother would ever get to be. My partner, a stay-at-home dad, a man who lived for his kids and enriched their childhoods in so many ways, there he is without the pain that now resides in his eyes. As for me, I barely recognize myself in the photos: who is that smiling woman? We have all changed individually, as a family, and in our relationships with one another. We tread carefully around each other, none of us wanting to disturb the fragile peace.

I met an old acquaintance recently who apologized for not

keeping in touch. She said she just didn't know what to say or what to do. I told her it's simple: just show up. You don't have to have any special words to say, just check in once in a while, meet me for tea or coffee. Don't expect me to be the one to take the initiative. I am afraid of putting people on the spot and can't bear rejection, intended or not. I cannot be certain that you want to hear from me or spend time with me now. I may be reluctant to commit to a date in the future, and usually give a conditional acceptance to invitations, as I am never sure when I might not be having a good day.

Here is what I would tell anyone interested in knowing: do not assume since time has gone by that we are fine (we never "get over it"); there is no closure when you lose a child. We learn after long years of trying to accept the cruel reality to live with our new (and diminished) life. For the most part we can cope, with the regular painful times bringing it all back, fresh and raw: the birthdays, holidays, the anniversary of the death, and any family gathering where our child is always going to be missing. Time is marked starkly for me as my son's friends get married and have children of their own, events I will never get to celebrate with him.

True support is showing up, being there for me, asking me what works the best for me. Letting me talk about my son. Contrary to what you might think, it isn't upsetting for me to talk about him, but avoiding it or changing the subject when I mention my son, well that really does upset me. Please address my loss, if you haven't already done so, because there is no expiry date on compassion, no rule about an appropriate timeframe to express your condolences. If you avoid mentioning my loss or my son, it hurts me. It is a big part of who I am now.

And I do have a life now, albeit a very different one from what I had imagined. It includes a deep appreciation and love for the people close to me, and it is emotionally rich and genuine. So who am I now?

I am a tougher, more resilient version of myself. Somehow, over time, I have managed to pick up the shattered, gutted bits left of me and reassemble them: I have no other choice but to carry on, but I do it more deliberately, with courage and determination. I recognize I am also more vulnerable; my emotions are much closer to the surface. I feel the pain of others more acutely, especially those who have lost children. I am also more grounded and realistic; I have learned to expect very little and appreciate the moments of happiness come my way. I am much wiser and better at putting things in perspective and concentrating my energy on what is truly important and meaningful for me. There is no amount of magical thinking that will bring my son back, no matter how much I dream of it or long for it. I must carry on, the best I can, for my family and for my dear sweet lost son.

## BACKSTORY

Jesse was a charismatic young man with a large personality; he always had an optimistic outlook and an exuberant sense of fun. In his twenty-seven years, he lived life to the fullest. Gregarious and outgoing, he had a wide circle of friends and touched all who met him. Though wise beyond his years, he struggled in school, and despite challenges, he managed to realize his dream of becoming a pilot earning both his private and commercial licenses.

Early in January 2009, Jesse, by then an experienced young pilot with over eight hundred hours in his log, crashed his four-seater airplane in the Laurentian Mountains. On a deliberate night flight, he was taking three friends to Saint John, New Brunswick. After refueling in Québec City and continuing the journey with a perfect weather forecast, he flew into a sudden freak snowsquall, lost all visual orientation, and crashed into the trees. We received a phone call at 6:30 in the morning that the plane had crashed. The rescue mission was a difficult one in a heavily forested area, and it wasn't until noon we learned the worst news—our son and his front seat passenger were dead. The two back seat passengers survived, one with only minor injuries.

Our story and our grief became very public. The media, chasing a potentially sensational story, descended on our home. Several reporters phoned or parked at the end of our (thankfully) long driveway. It was our desperate and painful task to reach family and close friends before they heard about it on the radio or television. The celebration of life event we held for Jesse in our small community attracted hundreds of people, including reporters. Not everything that was reported in the media was factual, yet we had to hold our heads up and try to carry on.

At that time, I had a very busy and demanding job as a manager of a public service department in a large academic library. Work became a welcome distraction. I found support through the Bereaved Families of Ontario, and the Ottawa-Outaouais chapter of The Compassionate Friends (TCF). For the past five years, I have been volunteering as a facilitator at our monthly TCF sharing circles, and I curate the chapter's lending library. By supporting more recently bereaved parents, I have found new purpose and a way to give back. As one further along in my grief journey, I can show by example that it is possible to function and even eventually find some enjoyment in life again.

# 25.
# Evensong

MARTHA ROYEA

Tonight, I took my son to the lake.

Song sparrows called from their evening perches,

tree to tree,
       tree to tree—

*O lord, open thou our lips.*
      *And our mouth shall show forth thy praise.*

Three years I have carried ashes in a small plastic film canister.

Now, it is empty.

(Cowichan Lake, July 2016)

# 26.
# Don't Worry about Getting Old, Mum

BONNIE WATERSTONE

"DON'T WORRY ABOUT getting old, Mum. I'll take care of you," my son David would say, bending down from his five foot eleven inches to my five foot two inches and hugging me. Smiling, I'd lean into him, hugging him back. His love was big; his heart was warm.

It's hard to write this. Oh, I can give the facts in a few words: my son David died on 13 December 2014, at the age of forty-four of a brain tumour (glioblastoma). The feelings, the stories, the witness to his life, and to how much we shared, however, that takes much more. And who or what can contain it? It's unfathomable, without limit.

When David was born, I was twenty-one years old and living in the Kootenays, a region with mountains, lakes and rivers in the interior of British Columbia. It was 1970, and David's father and I had come to British Columbia in late 1966. He had refused to fight in the Vietnam War, and like many displaced Americans who came to Canada at that time, we were part of the back-to-the-land hippie movement. David was born at home in a little cabin near the junction where the highway up the Slocan Valley begins—near Crescent Valley. When he died, he and his family—wife Laure and son Daniel—were living in Slocan Park, a fifteen-minute drive from where he was born. David and Laure had come there with their toddler and bought a piece of land to settle. They were coming back to the land, a different experience in 2006, but with a similar pull to the forests, mountains, and rivers, the wild beauty.

On 9 March 2014, I got a phone call from Laure. David had gone unconscious and was being rushed in an ambulance to the hospital. A CT scan revealed a brain tumour: he would have to have brain surgery immediately. The only symptoms he had had were headaches and nausea—similar to a flu—for about a week. The closest cancer centre was in Kelowna, a four-and-a-half hour drive away through mountainous country. My home is in Gibsons, a ferry ride away from Vancouver, on the Sunshine Coast. Dazed and in shock, I went to Vancouver and caught a bus to Kelowna. That bus ride was full of tears and prayers. I arrived on 10 March in the afternoon, just as David was waking up from surgery, his first moments of consciousness.

His wife and I were standing at the end of his bed, and David looked at us and said with a big smile, "I'm so lucky." We went to stand on each side of him, close. I remember holding his hand, my heart so full. I still marvel at David's first words—his gratitude and appreciation. That was to be a theme of his journey over the next nine months. The day he died, he was very weak, but still softly saying "thank you" to the nurses who cared for him at the small hospital in Nelson.

The next few days, I was in shock. The neurosurgeon came to the bedside and told David and us that he had glioblastoma; he hadn't been able to remove all the tumour, only to debulk it. If David gained enough strength to have radiation, that might buy him six to twelve months. I remember my tone of voice when I phoned David's childhood friend Jesse in Vancouver and told him, "This could be fatal"—I was in disbelief. A week later, David went unconscious again, and he was rushed for a CT scan. The neurosurgeon on call told Laure and me that he only had a few hours to live. We stayed by his bed. I remember saying and singing "David, you are loved; you are surrounded by love" over and over again. Amazingly, he woke up. That was the first of several times we would be told he only has a few hours.

As soon as David was strong enough, he went to the Nelson hospital about half an hour's drive from his home, and after a week, he went home to a hospital bed set up in the living room of their mobile home—the room had a big bay window looking out to the mountains and trees. My partner Trisha, who had come to live in the motel with me in Kelowna, followed along, and we stayed with friends in Nelson. I continued to stay; in fact, for the rest of that year, I lived mostly in the Kootenays, returning home occasionally. When the weather got warmer, I moved into a camper on the Slocan Park property, and stayed there until the fall, when David went into the hospital for the last time.

I remember how I would come up to David's bedside, and he would hold out his hand to me, palm up, and I would place my hand in his. It fit so well. We had shared this gesture for many years, and he continued to connect on this heart level, which showed the strong qualities he had: warmth and caring.

David did get strong enough for radiation, and we went back to Kelowna for several weeks in the spring. David and Laure had a motel room, and Trisha and I had another one. We used a lot of alternative healing to help through radiation and to help slow, and hopefully even eliminate, the growth of the tumour. Trisha and I made a healthy lunch every day in our motel room, and David and Laure would come for lunch. The amazing community of the Slocan Valley stepped up to help care for nine-year-old Daniel. Daniel got to keep many of his routines the same, and to play with his friends.

I remember walking with David in Kelowna and talking about spring, how the trees were changing. He had a degree in forestry and resource management from the University of California at Berkeley, and he would talk about the stages of the maple trees. When we went beside the river, he would critique the constructed salmon passage and point out how the larger river channel had been altered to suit human needs, not the salmon's.

After radiation, David went back to Slocan Park. Palliative care—which meant home support and homecare nurses — came to help, although since this was a rural area, it wasn't often. Laure had to manage his many daily medications. His blood had to be tested weekly. I helped. There was so much to do. I remember once thinking: when they talk about being at the bedside, they don't talk about the smell of vomit or the constant laundry. David's brain was affected, sometimes causing incontinence, and the radiation caused nausea. There was no dryer, so doing laundry was major. Sometimes I took loads into the laundromat in Nelson, a thirty-minute drive away.

Being at home was good in so many ways, but it was also challenging. There was a danger of seizures. Laure and I were on constant alert, someone needing to be with David at all times. When he got up from bed or from the kitchen table to walk to the bathroom, we were beside him or watching. He was a big guy, but Laure figured out ways to keep him from falling. When we went on walks, we took a folding chair, and if he got weak, he could sit down.

Twice more, in May and in June, it looked like David would not make it. In June, he had a series of seizures and falls, and became very weak. After seeing him resting in bed with difficulty breathing, the homecare nurse told us, "It won't be long now." But he came through, and I have a photo of him with one of the disposable pans for nausea on his head, joking around. Daniel put one on his head, too. We were all so happy to see David's smile again.

You already know the end of this story, but here are a few more memories. David had to go into hospital because he became very weak in late November. There were no hospice beds in Nelson, so he was in a regular room. We put photos around and brought healthy food in for him. I stayed with a friend and spent time at the hospital every day. Laure and I took shifts; she usually stayed overnight, as the hospital had put in an extra bed for her. Daniel came and played his guitar (he was just learning). I practised my ukulele. Most of the time, David was resting. I brought in music and a small portable speaker to play songs David liked—calming ambient music and Threshold Choir songs, and one of his favourite songs, "Somewhere over the Rainbow."

I feel blessed because I got to be there when David took his first breath as well as when he took his last. Those last few days, which of course we did not know were the last few days, he was not talking much. On 13 December, Laure phoned, and I held the phone up so he could hear. The last words she said to him were "I love you" and he said, as strong as he could, "yes." A nurse came in to check on him and wash him up a bit. David said softly "thank you" as he usually did to the nurses; he often remembered their names, saying thank you Chuck, Cheryl, or whoever.

Lunch came, and I got ready to start helping him eat. He began to twitch and I thought *he's having a seizure*. So I pushed the button to call a nurse. Things happened very fast. Soon he was having trouble breathing, taking big difficult breaths like gulps. I was beside him, holding his hand and touching him. I said, "It's okay, you can let go, it's okay, you can let go, we love you." Maybe I said other things too, reassuring myself as much as him, but that's what I remember. Then suddenly, no more breath.

By that time, the room was filled with medical personnel. It turned out that the doctor on call was the younger son of my close friend with whom I was staying. I looked up from David's face and saw him on the other side of the bed, also leaning down close—"Lee!" I said. That was another blessing because he made the room peaceful and quiet, and he let us have many hours together. He phoned and talked with Laure.

That was the beginning of a long journey, which I am still on. Life without David is still unimaginable to me. I still want to hold his hand, to feel his hug, to hear his voice, and to laugh with him. He was in the habit for years of phoning me regularly. Now, I can hardly believe he won't phone and tell me how he's doing—he shared his feelings, his frustrations, his successes and enthusiasms, and his ideas. Can I live without that? It's a question for me still, and this is 2016. Not yet two years since he died. But I am still raw. I feel hollowed out. What's life all about, I wonder?

I am lucky. I have support, a loving partner, and friends. I have a community with an active hospice and a Compassionate Friends group. Friends who are in the Threshold Choir came and sang for me exactly one month after David died. I cried the whole time. I'm crying now as I write this. It's still just too hard.

I never thought I'd have to face life without David. He gave me so much and taught me so much. I was young when I had him, and he was the first person I truly loved. He stretched my heart. As a child, he was wise and funny and caring. He had a lot of courage—to be his own unique self. Especially as a teenager that was difficult, but he had an inner strength and integrity. Despite the separation that happened through divorce and unwise choices I made, David and I healed our relationship. I credit him with that. He came to live in Vancouver when he was twenty-eight. I was there going to university. One day, driving in his car with him, I was probably saying how I had to get home to study. He pulled quickly into a parking lot and said firmly, "Mum, you and I need to work on our relationship. You are going to spend time with me every week." Yes, he made it happen, and we became very close. Another memory from that time was watching a sunset with him and again, I was feeling as if I had to get busy—a theme for me. He said again: "No, you have time to watch a sunset with me." It is one of the many lessons from David that has changed my life. I now really know that beautiful sunsets and connecting with those you love are what's important.

I am still in grief. The loss is still crippling. At the beginning, I walked and walked every day. Then, three months after David's death, I injured my left foot. I haven't been able to walk well since then. It's better than it was, when I could only walk a few steps, and now I can go without crutches. But it was part of not being able to move forward. How can life go on? Why is it going on?

But I am beginning to be able to see my way. Meditation, keeping as healthy as possible, connecting with friends, keeping up my relationship with David's son Daniel, who is like him in many ways, reaching out for support—all this helps. And right now, I feel the sunshine coming in the window, and I'm going to wipe my tears and stop writing this.

David, I honour you and love you with all my heart.

# 27.
# Joy Reclaimed — Twenty Years After

CATHY SOSNOWSKY

O UR SON DIED TWENTY YEARS AGO today, tonight, actually, around midnight. His father Woldy and I have had nineteen times to practise living through his death anniversary—the worst day of our lives. I remember lying on Alex's bed on the first anniversary, determined to stay awake to prevent the knock at the door at midnight. When that knock came, we had been asleep. If we had stayed awake, could we have saved him? Of course not. He and his best friend, whose family Alex was staying at the Whistler ski resort, climbed a tennis bubble around 11:00 p.m. when they were out walking the family dog. The seam Alex stood on when they reached the top was weak. It ripped, and he fell to his death. Jonny managed to grab a cable on his way down, and he was only bruised. A freak accident. Two seventeen-year-old boys being adventurous—doing what they weren't supposed to do. Twenty years later, I still find it hard to believe that it really happened.

This morning—the twelfth day of the twelfth month, and, in this case, the twelfth year of this century (2012)—I spent writing Christmas cards and composing cheery notes about adjusting to our new life in the little town of Salmon Arm. Woldy was in his downstairs den, writing a sermon—a sermon for next Sunday, the third Sunday of Advent with the traditional theme of joy. How to be joyful on the anniversary of our son's death?

Woldy suddenly emerged from the basement and said, "I need to go for a walk. Do you want to come?"

"Just let me finish these last two cards, and I'll be with you."

Along the bird path edging Shuswap Lake, it's easy to get a rhythm, a good pace. Yesterday's snowfall had been padded down by other feet, by duck feet even. It was so sweet to see bird footprints on the bird path. We paced along, heads down, which were raised only occasionally by birdcalls from the bushes. We each knew that the other was thinking similar thoughts—thoughts about Alex, thoughts about surviving twenty years without him.

"I'm walking with bated breath," I finally said, breaking our silence.

"What? Why?"

"I'm wondering when you're going to ask me for lunch."

"Do we have time?"

"Yes, we have an hour till it's time to pick up Ainsley."

Parents again in our seventies, raising a now eleven-year-old granddaughter, Woldy with a new career as church minister, we have little time to spend with each other.

I chose my favourite pub-restaurant, the only one in town situated right by the lake. I love looking out its windows at the serene lakes-cape, backed by mountains and pierced frequently by bird flight.

Woldy ordered the day's special, soup and sandwich; he declined my suggestion that we order calamari in Alex's stead. It was one of the many dishes he loved. I ordered it for myself. We had fallen silent while waiting for our food, so I pulled out a little red note-book I carry in my purse.

"Let's do one of my journal writing exercises. We'll each list ten blessings Alex gave us, and then compare them." (It's hard to really retire from being an English teacher!)

I tore out two pages for Woldy, dug out two pens from my purse, and we set to it. We each reached ten before our lunches arrived. Between bites, we took turns sharing our lists and telling little anecdotes with them ("Remember the time..."). Alex's capacity for joy was on the top of both our lists. And both lists included gifts from Alex after he left us—compassion, tolerance, and hope.

Some of you reading this may be new to the long hard journey of grieving, and cannot believe joy will ever return to your lives. Have faith, I believe it will.

# 28.
# In Memory

BARB HAYDUK

*Days like this that I wish that I came home to you*
*This unceremonious goodbye just won't do*
*My anonymous work fades away like footsteps in the sand*
*Was I here, was I real, did you plan for all of this to end....*
—Chris Hayduk-Costa, "Pale Blue Dot," 2012

WHY AM I WRITING this? I remember being there. I remember what it felt like at the early stages of losing a child. Grief is a journey, and I can speak about where it has taken me and where I am today.

I learned other people may understand loss, but if they have not lost a child, they will not understand. I get that now. I was one of them before—thinking that in time, those poor parents will move on. What I understand now is, yes, bereaved parents move forward, but they hold their child in their hearts and keep a relationship with him or her for as long as they live.

11 September is a day etched in the minds of many. For me, it is a day emblazoned in my soul for an additional reason: on this day in 2012, my beautiful twenty-five-year-old son Chris Hayduk-Costa died.

I married Chris's dad, Manuel, in 1986, and a year later, Chris was born followed by our daughter Gabrielle, three years later. From the beginning, Chris and Gab enjoyed a healthy sibling bond.

Chris was an extraordinary, gifted young man, with a spark for life. He had a love for his family and friends, an enormous passion for music, a quick wit, a positive attitude, and a soft spot in his heart for pets. He was authentic and accepted himself for who he was; he was not interested in changing to please others.

Chris was born with several health challenges that required surgeries and treatments over the years. Despite these, he possessed an inner light, and charmed people with his precociousness and sense of humour. As a child, he loved to laugh and sing, and he adored being around people. He made good friends from kindergarten throughout his primary school years; he nourished these friendships right up until his death.

At the age of fourteen, Chris's love for music led him to the music program at Canterbury High School, which has a highly regarded fine arts program. Shortly after starting grade nine, however, Chris was diagnosed with an aggressive form of non-Hodgkin's lymphoma, Burkitt's lymphoma. He underwent a whirlwind of surgeries and chemotherapy treatments. We were shocked and blindsided by this life-threatening diagnosis, and before Chris's death, I would have described that period as being the most difficult we had ever faced, as we had to visit the possibility of losing him. His illness, no doubt, contributed to his values and priorities—such as his family and friends and living in the moment. It had a deep impact on me as well.

At the age of twenty, Chris was diagnosed with partial complex seizures, a form of epilepsy. Although he had navigated his other health challenges well, this diagnosis hit him hard. He commented to me how upset he was with the hand dealt to him, regarding his health. Something seemed to happen to him every five years. The neurologist advised that with medication, his epilepsy was manageable. He never mentioned that epilepsy could be fatal or what could be done to reduce that risk. This is something I continue to struggle with today. With medication, Chris's epilepsy seemed to be nonexistent as he became seizure free. I reminded him that the five-year intervals of bad luck with his health were purely coincidence. In hindsight, this conversation seemed like a foreshadowing of what was to come.

Chris's life was blossoming as he completed an honour's BA in international business and was working at the Library of Parliament, while continuing to pursue his passion in music. As a vocalist, pianist, guitarist, bassist and drummer, he played in several bands, wrote music, recorded songs, and enjoyed playing gigs.

We were privileged that Chris prioritized family and friends, as he rarely missed family events and continued to join me on vacations. I did not take this for granted, as I, too, was imprinted with Chris's cancer journey. Having shared these experiences, I have an odd just-in-time feeling.

In 2012, Chris moved into his ultimate bachelor pad. It was a pleasure to see him so content with life. That time coincided with me taking initial steps to retire from the Royal Canadian Mounted Police after thirty-two years of service. While enjoying my last weeks of work, I received an urgent phone call informing me Chris had not shown up for work that day (12 September 2012) or the day before. My mother's intuition told me that something was seriously wrong, as it was not like Chris to miss work without notifying his employer. I called Manuel and Gab, who in turn made additional inquiries with Chris's friends and roommate. I left my office and drove to his apartment. I remember my feeling of panic and thinking of the discussion I would have with Chris about how worried he had us while we were trying to locate him—a conversation I would never get to have.

Chris's roommate said he had last seen Chris the evening of 10 September when they had watched television together. They worked at different places, had their own friends, different schedules, and because Chris had the master bedroom with an ensuite, his roommate had not seen him since that night. He said that Chris's bedroom door had been closed. Because his roommate was at work, he buzzed me remotely into the building. I knocked on the apartment door, but no answer. I went to the parking garage where I found Chris's car. I immediately knew the significance of that. I was so scared of what I might find. I drove to his roommate's place of work to pick up his apartment key. All the while, I was filled with a sense of dread. I opened the apartment door, knocked on Chris's bedroom door, no answer; then, I slowly opened the door, saw that his bed was empty but the light in the ensuite bathroom was on. I thought I saw some vapour on the mirror in the washroom, and my first thought was "oh good he was just in the shower." I called out to Chris, but there was no answer. I pushed the door open further and saw him on the floor. It was obvious to me that he could not be resuscitated.

I struggle to this day with my reaction to finding Chris. I understood he was dead, and I went into my police mode calling 911, which began the parade of police, paramedics, and the coroner. I know I was in shock, and my heart had not caught up. The scene was surreal, as though it really couldn't be happening. I did not cry; I did not scream. I was on auto pilot. Today, when I think about that moment, I am sickened by it. My visceral reaction accompanying those thoughts is like one that would normally be expected on finding him compared to how I was when I actually found him.

I was worried about everyone else, except me. Manuel called. I ensured he was sitting down and he had someone with him when I told him the news that would change our lives forever. He said he was coming over, and I insisted he be driven. When Gab called me, I had to remain calm so as not to convey the situation, not wanting her to be alone to receive the news. I asked Gab to meet Manuel and me at the apartment. I called a colleague and informed her about Chris; I requested she close up my things at the office, but I asked she not share the news. How bizarre was that? It was as though I subconsciously felt that by not telling people, then it didn't happen. When Gab arrived at the building, we met her in the lobby. I will never forget hearing Gab's piercing screams as they echoed through the lobby upon learning about Chris. We had to physically help her up to the apartment where we waited with the police for the coroner.

The coroner examined the scene and said she suspected Chris died from sudden unexpected death in epilepsy, SUDEP. I blurted out something to the effect that we were never told about SUDEP, to which she responded, "Why would we tell someone they could die from the condition if there is nothing they can do about it?" I later learned this was not accurate, but it did not change our reality. One of the attending police officers, knowing my profession, said to me, "You are going to crash later." I actually said I knew it. In addition to my shock and my police autopilot mode, I was subconsciously trying to keep my emotions under control until I didn't have to. I was also worried about Chris's roommate who was still at work.

After Chris's body was collected, it was time for us to leave. We could not absorb what was happening: Gab was discussing whether or not she would be able to make it to her lab at the university that evening, and Manuel was talking about going into work the following day. Although earlier I was adamant that Manuel not drive, I did not follow my own advice. We left Chris's apartment in a total daze, and I drove Gab to the university, although Gab was finally convinced by a friend not to attend the lab session. I dropped Manuel at his place and then went home with Gab. When I walked into the house, I broke down. My memory of the rest of that evening is patchy.

## LIFE AFTER

I felt as if I moved in a fog for the weeks following Chris's death. Because it was sudden and unexpected, I felt blindsided. We all build our lives on fundamental assumptions, and in my case, I assumed I would witness and enjoy seeing Chris experience many more milestones as he had so much more living to do. My foundation of assumptions had come crumbling down. I loved my role as a mother, and I felt it was the most important responsibility I had. Having nurtured Chris through his health challenges and then losing him without warning felt as if the bottom had dropped out. What was the point of life? Of everything?

I never envisioned making funeral arrangements for my child or choosing a casket, an urn, or deciding whether to cremate or bury my son, or deciding what to write for his obituary. It was all so surreal in the absolute worst way, a nightmare, one I could not awaken from. For the visitation at the funeral home and Chris's celebration of life, it was like moving through a dream state. I was aware of what was happening—wishing I could just stop every-thing. I went through the motions, but I could not fully grasp the extent of our loss. It all felt unreal.

For months, Chris's death did not compute. I often felt I could not catch my breath and had a knot in my stomach whenever my thoughts went to Chris, which was almost all the time. I thought about how positively pissed off Chris would have been had he known his life would be cut short. I had insomnia, and only slept a few hours a night. When I would wake up, for a split second, I would think all was well, but then I would remember Chris had died.

Chris's death changed me. At times I didn't care about anything including myself—that is, with the exception of Gab. I did not care about eating. When I went for a run, I welcomed the feeling of extreme fatigue because I could focus on a discomfort other than my pain of losing Chris. I was not suicidal, but my will to live diminished. I did not have tolerance for hearing about trivial complaints of others. I hated hearing the news and television in general. I didn't want to know about the troubles of the world. It was hard to see life continue for everyone else, and I wanted to scream "Don't you realize that Chris died?" My world revolved around my loss. I questioned what life was about. We are born, and then at some point, we die. Why do we do what we do? Before Chris died, I would have described myself as being a positive, happy, grateful person. I almost never cried. That was the before me. Afterward, everything reminded me of Chris, and I repeatedly relived my loss.

I lost a lot of confidence in myself and in life. I had believed that if we lived well, with strong values, essentially, if we did the right things, then life would unfold positively. Chris's death shook my whole foundation of truths. It is humbling to finally really understand at the ripe old age of fifty-two how little control of our lives we have.

Within a few weeks, through the fog and with a great deal of anguish, I packed up Chris's belongings from his apartment, and with the help of family and friends, we moved them back home. We still have not done anything with his effects. I really don't know if we ever will. There is no timeline. I began cancelling Chris's accounts, which was like closing Chris down. Although I felt competent when I was working, after Chris died, doing this task felt insurmountable. On numerous occasions, I broke down on the phone when explaining the circumstances.

What kept me moving forward after Chris died was being able to focus on Gabrielle by supporting and looking after her. She was dealing with losing her brother while navigating medical school applications and her fourth year of university. Gabrielle gave me a purpose and a reason to get up every morning.

Through my journey, I have learned that everyone's grief is unique, and, consequently, we all require a unique approach to moving forward. After Chris died, I felt a strong need to be understood. I needed to convince myself what I was experiencing was normal. I wasn't going crazy.

## POSITIVE STEPS

There were a few steps I took that helped me even in my darkest moments. For more than a year after losing Chris, I attended a few monthly bereavement support groups, including those held by Compassionate Friends—an organization providing emotional support for parents who have lost a child. I found it comforting to have my feelings validated by others who were walking the same path, although I had hopes my feelings would be temporary and I would "get over" this loss.

Eventually, I formed a closed bereavement group with other parents who had lost a child. It provided an environment free from judgment, where we shared personal stories and feelings without censoring ourselves. Many people are uncomfortable hearing about such a loss, and it causes them to avoid the topic. Avoiding the situation for me was like ignoring the biggest part of my life. It took so much energy to pretend. Such was not the case with this group. We rarely offered wisdom or advice but instead provided understanding and support.

In addition to the bereavement groups, I sought counselling from a psychologist on and off for the first few years. This was my subconscious attempt to find what I had lost, but that was not going to happen. At different times, I thought I should be able to "fly solo" and manage without the help of a professional. Eventually, I realized I still needed the support. In time, I became strong enough to carry on without the assistance.

For months, I found solace in reading books and articles about loss, loss of a child, and sudden loss. I again received validation that what I was feeling and going through were normal. I also learned how others dealt with their loss and continued to move ahead each day, and I learned how the loss of a child is not the same as other losses. The death of one's child does not compute as part of our life assumptions. When it happens, it takes years to understand it.

I found grieving my child to be particularly isolating. Because most people don't understand the breadth and depth of losing a child, their tolerance for grief wanes with time. I began to hide my emotions by wearing a mask, something that is exhausting. I appeared to function on the surface, but I hid my feeling of disconnectedness. I could not actively engage in discussions about superficial issues, and I closed in on myself leaving room for only a select few. What helped to pull me out of myself was getting a rescue poodle that needed a lot of attention and socialization. Meeting other dog owners helped me to reconnect. I had no choice really if I was to help my new dog. It is difficult to discern who rescued whom.

Living purposefully has been another focus that has helped me deal with my reality of Chris's death. It took almost ten months to receive the coroner's report confirming SUDEP was the cause of death. Although it was mentioned at the earliest stages of the death investigation, it really did not make sense to me, as it had never been mentioned by Chris's neurologist. Chris had been cancer free for more than ten years with no sign of relapse, so I could not understand how he could just die suddenly. I felt strongly compelled to understand why and how he died. I connected with SUDEP organizations, researchers, politicians, public servants, doctors, and other bereaved families. I attended international epilepsy conferences and held a fundraiser.

When I learned Chris's death might have been avoided had his doctor informed him about the risk and ways to reduce his risk, I knew I could contribute to educating others. I was really channelling my anger at the situation to do something worthwhile. At the same time, this has been difficult for me as with every step I take, I revisit my loss. I do it in my son's memory. That is what drives me.

I also volunteer with the Children's Wish Foundation of Canada. I do this too in honour of Chris, since he would have done if he were still with us. It was his favourite charity as he received a wish following his cancer. He also received the Queen's Diamond Jubilee Medal posthumously for his volunteer efforts with the organization.

In the past, I had reflected, as most of us do, on what life is really about, but Chris's death brought about a greater depth of existential crisis than I had ever previously experienced. Losing my child made me wonder what my life, my efforts, and relationships had all been for. The need to live purposefully has been helpful in integrating Chris's death into my life.

I created a scholarship in Chris's name, which is awarded annually to a graduating fine arts student at the high school he attended. It reassured me that people would remember Chris as it exemplifies the attributes and values he possessed. It is important for me that people know he mattered, he was here, and his death was not in vain. I want him to be remembered and to ensure his legacy is perpetuated. I also had a commemorative bench and tree installed in a city park in his memory.

Although some find it difficult to look at pictures and videos of their child who has died, I tend to immerse myself in them around the difficult anniversaries. Over the years, I have created memorial calendars, books, and videos about Chris, which I have shared with family and friends.

## UNHELPFUL

When there is a death, I have found some people assume that others share the same belief system and try to console with their religious-based comments. Some, knowing that I am an atheist, tell me Chris is watching over me, he is proud of me, God only gives us what we can handle, or he is in a better place. They say God has his arms open to me, they say God bless you, and they pray for Chris. I know it brings them comfort, but I find no relief in their words. I remind myself that those offering these "blessings" are doing so from a caring place; however, I cannot help but feel my beliefs have not been respected. I respond with a thank you, yet their comments do not bring the result they hoped. For me, Chris lived, he died, and he will not experience life anymore. I do not believe I will see Chris again. I do not believe his spirit is living in another dimension. For me, his life is over, and he is no more. I wish I could believe otherwise, but I don't.

Another difficult aspect has been when people offer me advice about my need to move on and what I should be feeling. Interestingly enough, this advice has never been from a parent who has lost a child. Essentially the message I receive is that I was "grieving wrong." Losing Chris affected my self-confidence, and this further compounded my insecurity, as I tended to reflect on their opinions in case there was some legitimacy to them. That said, in hindsight, I realize I was doing as well as could be expected.

## MULTIPLE LOSSES

The year following Chris's death coincided with a number of personal life changes and losses that pale in comparison to losing Chris but contributed to complicating and extending my grief.

After thirty-two years with the RCMP, I was planning my retirement; I had submitted my papers and then Chris died. The day I found Chris became my last day of work. Retirement for some is a transition, and for some, it represents a loss of identity. I no longer had the social contact of work and was no longer an employee for an organization that may have had an interest in my wellbeing. Though much less significant, I was also robbed of the retirement celebration that then I did not want.

One of the most difficult secondary losses I experienced was the relationship with my mother following Chris's death. Although my mother and I purchased a house together after my separation from my ex-husband, my mother was self-medicating with alcohol; she had been hostile to Chris and was continuing to be emotionally abusive to Gab. I was no longer capable of duct taping the relationship and caring for her when I needed to protect Gab, and I needed to grieve. I moved out of our home for the remainder of Gab's school year, after which Gab moved away to study medicine. The bond I had with my mother was forever changed, as she was very hostile about my decision to prioritize Gab and myself. This situation coincided with my becoming an "empty nester," which can be difficult even under the best of circumstances.

Within seven months of losing Chris, our fifteen-year-old family dog had to be put down, which brought fresh grief to the surface again. When I cried at the loss of Westa, I was crying for Chris too.

I believe I would have accepted each of these less significant losses sooner, but given Chris's death, they brought on fresh tears for him.

I still think of Chris throughout my days, as almost everything reminds me of him. The list seems endless. Whether it is hearing a song on the radio, eating a favourite meal, seeing his old room, driving by his old haunts, grocery shopping, seeing a young child, teenager, or young adult who possess some similarity to him, the memories are conjured up. I have a sadness at family events because of his absence; I revere the birthdays he is no longer celebrating, and I honour the anniversary of his death. The lead up to these difficult dates continues to be more difficult than the days themselves. I never feel I have adequately and appropriately marked these days as nothing feels right. Seeing my son's friends move on, complete their education, settle into careers, marry, and start families makes me sad Chris will never have those opportunities, nor will he share in the joy of his friends' milestones. This remains bittersweet.

On my last Mother's Day with Chris, knowing that I was close to retiring, he gave me a framed picture with the words "Live Today." It really is about the journey and not the destination because life can change in an instant. My advice for others is hug your loved ones—everyday if you can. Tell them you love them often and don't put off or take for granted any opportunities to be with them. No one knows the future.

As I am writing this today, I am four years along since Chris died. In this time, the magnitude of my grief has softened, and the frequency has lessened. I continue to learn to ride the wave. It will never disappear. He is never far from my thoughts. I will always hold Chris close to my heart.

In Loving Memory of Chris Hayduk-Costa
3 September 1987 – 11 September 2012
*Our Light, Our Laughter and Our Song*

# 29.
## However Did We Survive?

ANDY BOND

MANY PEOPLE, POSSIBLY MOST, have experienced the death of a loved one—perhaps a spouse, parent, brother or sister, or close friend—and understand that the death of someone you love changes you. But the extent of the change when that loved one is your child is almost impossible to imagine. When a child dies, parents experience intense emotions—shock, anger, denial, perhaps guilt for not sufficiently caring for or protecting the child, disorientation for outliving their child, and a shattering of dreams for the child. Disruptive changes occur in the family structure, as a younger child becomes the eldest or a middle child is suddenly missing.

When our son died, we became part of a group no one wants to join, a group based on a shared terrible experience. The tragedy that links the parents is something that no one would choose to experience.

In October 1994, my wife and I experienced this turmoil firsthand when a police constable arrived on our doorstep at 2:30 in the morning to tell us that our twenty-year-old son, Kevin, had died. What he actually said was "he had stopped breathing at 12:03 a.m." Kevin was starting his second year at Trent University and had just returned to Peterborough from a camping trip during reading week. We had bought him a new tent and sleeping bag for his twentieth birthday and given them to him when he was home for Thanksgiving just two weeks earlier. He collapsed after a hard cycle ride with a friend. Fortunately, his friend had taken CPR training during a summer tree-planting job, but unfortunately, his efforts were unsuccessful. We spent many weeks speculating on the circumstances. Had Kevin accidentally taken something toxic? Did the chocolate bar he ate while travelling contain bad peanuts? Did he contract beaver fever or some other virus while he was camping? And so on and so on.

After several months, the coroner informed us that the likely cause of Kevin's death was a cardiac arrhythmia resulting from an enlarged heart—a condition "not compatible with life." He noted that there are often no warnings with this condition and that the first symptom is usually death. We continued to speculate on what might have caused his heart to enlarge; we investigated many possibilities, and we underwent tests to see whether we or our other children had the same condition. Heart specialists and the Ontario Coroner felt that the most likely cause was a Cox-Sackie virus, but they could offer no theories as to where this virus might have come from. Eventually, with no clear answers, we ran out of possibilities and had to accept that Kevin's death resulted from a random combination of factors and that we will never know for sure what happened.

This questioning seems to be a common reaction to the death of a child, particularly if the death was sudden or unexpected. Parents may examine and relive the circumstances and agonize over the whys and what ifs. Although friends are expecting closure, it may take years to come to accept the fact of a child's death and to think about moving forward.

I have learned there is no such thing as closure: the death has happened. There is no going back, and it is now part of who I am. A more appropriate term is "acceptance," in which the emotional heart can eventually catch up to the rational brain. The journey to emotional acceptance is personal and hard. There is no going under or around this grief work, only going through it. It is frightening, exhausting, and can feel like you're going crazy.

Our initial reaction to the news was to consider driving the four hours to the hospital in Peterborough. The constable persuaded us instead to call the duty physician for additional information. He confirmed our son's identity and that neither alcohol nor drugs were involved, but he could not provide further details of the circumstances. After this call, we just sat for hours waiting for a reasonable time to call our families overseas and our daughter who was at university in Hamilton. We left our twelve-year-old son asleep upstairs.

The next forty-eight hours were mostly a blur. Friends stopped by, family members arrived from overseas, and we started to make plans for Kevin's funeral. After running on shock, no food or sleep for several days, we had an emotional crash as reality finally registered.

We managed to get through the funeral, collect Kevin's effects from his apartment in Peterborough and even start to work again. My wife went back to her work as the office manager for a small business as she found the routine allowed her to function even while constantly thinking of Kevin. I had been laid off in September, so my focus was back on the job search, which involved a lot of time at home. Eventually, in February 1995, I secured a senior management position, but I found the transition extremely challenging because of the combination of learning a new business and my depleted emotional energy level.

Over the several months after Kevin's death, we were extremely grateful for the emotional and practical support we received from friends and neighbours, our church, and our community groups as well as the casseroles that just showed up in the fridge, the phone calls, and the cards of sympathy. Eventually, the casseroles ran out, and the visitors—with one notable exception—stopped coming as frequently, as they hoped that we were "over it." Despite their best intentions, they could not begin to understand the impact that Kevin's early death had on my wife and me, his older sister and younger brother—both as a family and as individuals. Nor did we know what to expect as we started on our individual grief journeys.

My wife and I avidly read everything we could find on grieving. We quickly found a notable difference between books and articles written by or for psychologists, counsellors, doctors, and researchers, and those written by parents who had actually experienced the loss of a child. The first ones were objective, analytical; the others spoke from the heart. When we compared notes, my wife and I found that even these authors spoke to us differently in our personal journeys. My most meaningful author was Jim Taylor, a bereaved father and United Church minister from British Columbia. His work, however, did not resonate as well with my wife, as she preferred a different style. This was one of the early realizations that although we were grieving together, we were on separate paths.

We attended meetings of the Bereaved Families of Ontario and made contact with other grieving parents. Our daughter, whom we mistakenly sent back to university in Hamilton one week after her brother died, did her own research and put us in touch with The Compassionate Friends in Winnipeg. In the fall of 1998, we attended their National Conference in Kelowna, British Columbia, and in early 1999, with two other bereaved parents, we started a chapter in Ottawa.

It is now twenty-three years since Kevin died. We began our journey into the dark fog of grief, not knowing where we were, where we were going, or what was ahead of us. The first few years were very stressful on the whole family, as we tried to come to terms with life without our middle son. My wife and I were on tenterhooks around each other, as we each dealt differently with our grief. Our daughter somehow managed to keep things together enough to complete her final university year, then left for a position in Toronto, as living at home was almost unbearable for her. Our younger son was devastated by the sudden loss of his hockey and music buddy. For months, he slept on the floor in our bedroom so as not to be alone in his room.

The relationship with some of our other family members came under great stress with the suggestion that Kevin's cardiomyopathy could be genetic and the inference that his death might somehow have been their fault. Although some friends understood, others talked about their children's progress without realizing the pain this caused us. We developed several coping mechanisms: lighting a small candle for Kevin whenever we had family occasions; giving each other space to grieve as we felt appropriate; and parking at the end of the driveways when we went to get-togethers at friends' homes so that we could leave early if conversation became difficult, or if we strongly felt the awkward elephant in the room—where people avoided talking about our son while we wanted them to talk to us about him.

We were fortunate we did not have to deal with any legal issues involving the justice system, as these processes can take years to resolve and cause additional stress. Even so, it was seven years before we started to feel we could begin to move forward with our lives without feeling we were forgetting Kevin. We joined a hiking club that resulted in a new appreciation for the outdoors, and we worked on developing the Ottawa chapter of The Compassionate Friends. This allowed us to turn our grief toward a positive experience by sharing with other bereaved parents.

Part of the enduring legacy of Kevin's death has been this increased desire to give back by helping others. Our work with The Compassionate Friends lets us give back. In addition to overseeing the Ottawa Chapter, we have joined the National Board and support chapters across the country. I am thankful that despite an extremely stressful journey, the resulting change for our family was not toward negativity, depression, and loss of hope; we have thus far been able to follow a path toward positive reconciliation of grief, with a new appreciation of life and its mysteries. I am thankful, too, that with time we survived this devastating blow, and we emerged stronger for it. I believe that is due in no small part to our involvement with The Compassionate Friends.

Both my wife and I changed careers. After more than thirty years in the technology industry, I moved into the field of career transition and retirement planning. Based on my experience of corporate reorganizations and layoffs and my personal journey following the death of my son, I found it rewarding to help others come to grips with life transitions. My wife moved from managing a small private business to being office manager at a long-term care facility. This allowed her to use her professional skills while providing care and support to others.

Our daughter is pursuing a professional career; she is married with two children who are learning about their Uncle Kevin. Our son is pursuing his passion as a musician and sound recording engineer and producer. Kevin is still very much part of our lives today. We celebrate his birthday with a family dinner and acknowledge his death day with a visit to Algonquin Park where his ashes are scattered. We contribute to the Trans-Canada Trail in his memory and have plaques in several locations across the country where he visited. Our friends contributed to a memorial plaque in the Algonquin Park Visitor Centre, and we have donated benches to our local park where Kevin used to play as a child.

Although we would not have chosen this life path, we are grateful we have survived the journey with a new appreciation of life and an acceptance of death as part of the natural cycle. I hope sharing our story provides some encouragement for other bereaved parents on their grief journey.

# 30.
# Daniel

SYLVIA PASHER

Until now, I have not been able to write about Daniel. My head and heart are full of thoughts of him, of the worries over the years, of the funny stories, of the difficulties we endured together, of the love we had for him. I am in awe of the person who lived outside our family, the person I knew only as a son. When I think of him my tears flow freely, and, sometimes, like right now, I cannot see the computer screen.

I always knew that Daniel was much more than the boy I watched over and struggled with right from his birth. Daniel was always different, always unique, and as his parent, I was at a loss to know how to deal with him and how to help him to live in this world. I felt I was not up to the job of mothering such an intelligent, gifted, creative, yet difficult child. My heart ached for the little boy who was left out. At age two, he questioned us about death, at four, he could not understand social hypocrisy, at eight, he asked to talk to a counsellor because he wasn't happy, and at ten, he could say of a classmate "he's not as nice as his mother thinks he is."

As his mother, it was my job to worry; that's what mothers do. (Daniel knew that, and I think he appreciated it.) Would he ever find a place for himself in this world? Would he ever be accepted by others? Would he find a Jewish community where he would fit in as a fundamentalist? Would he meet a girl to love and who would love him as he was? Would he succeed in holding a research and teaching position in Jerusalem, the city of his birth? Would his illnesses prevent him from doing what others do?

It was to his parents he turned when he was overwhelmed by his health problems. It was his dad who received the call when he was twenty-five to please come and get him because he was unwell. It was his family who saw him immobilized, unable to get off the floor, unable to do anything, and it was his brother who often bore the brunt of his pain. To read how each friend, colleague, and teacher expressed that Daniel never used his illness as an excuse, never told them how sick he was, or never let on how invasive the condition was or how debilitating is a revelation to his family. We didn't know that outside the home he conquered his illnesses to the best of his ability. At home, he allowed himself to be weak, he allowed himself to despair, he allowed himself to lean on us, and he allowed his anger to show. We would have liked to get to know the man the world met. We shall never have this opportunity.

Daniel, I have stopped worrying about you, but I shall never stop thinking about you.

Daniel: Jerusalem 1978 – Ottawa 2005

# 31.
# The Bird

JUDITH MAGUET

I WAS THE YOUNGEST OF FIVE, and favoured by my dad. At the age of twelve, my dad left us, and I felt if he didn't love me enough to stay, no one could love me, not even me.

After five years, my mother remarried, and she and I moved from Vancouver Island to the isolated area of Reykjavik, Manitoba. Leaving extended family, friends, and familiar territory behind was difficult for me. My stepfather had been a longtime bachelor and had lived in a comfortable but basic home. He was a cattle rancher; he protected the Canada geese on his lakefront property, and he offered security and kindness. He was "good stuff."

During the first summer, we lived at the Reykjavik ranch. At night in my bedroom, I used to hear the whip-poor-will calling again and again. It sounded to me like a message of "all is well, all is well." It was peaceful.

In the basement of the house, tucked in a corner, was an old metal bed. When I fell in love with a farmer who lived an hour's drive away, whenever it was too late for him to drive home from our ranch, he slept in that bed in the basement. But one morning, like a prospector, he chipped off enough paint to discover the base of the bed was solid brass. After our wedding, this brass bed was moved to our home, the farm. The sentimental value it holds has kept it as an important piece of our forty-year marriage. The labour of love that uncovered the gleaming beauty remains as an added element to its value.

For the past thirty-seven years, I have lived on our farm near Ste. Rose, an hour from the ranch. My husband has never lived anywhere but here, and neither of us has ever heard a whip-poor-will at our home. Here is where we raised our two sons and our daughter.

Several years ago, I admired my very talented friend's handmade quilt. I hinted to my husband that I would love one of her quilts. Unbeknownst to me, he tried to hire her to make a quilt for me, but with her many children and grandchildren, she said she would be busy for years making each of them a quilt.

After my stepfather and mother passed away, the treasured Reykjavik ranch bed took on an even greater significance, as an important link for me to the ranch. Eventually the ranch, itself a close tie to my parents, became our son's ranch.

On 11 June 2007, our son was killed in a crash while piloting his private airplane over West Hawk Lake. Our Joel, our second son, our Reykjavik rancher. The pain was unbearable. Life became very difficult after that. And to make it worse, the media coverage was incredibly hurtful. It felt like life could not be endured.

## THE BIRD

At 2:45 a.m. on the second night after Joel died, I was woken by a whip-poor-will calling loudly through our open bedroom window. Sitting up in bed, I listened to it for a long time.

In the morning, I told my husband and our daughter about the bird and about how I had never heard its call except from my little bedroom at Reykjavik. They listened to my story, and our day went on with the nightmare we had to get through.

The next evening, we were up late with the many visitors who had come to offer their much needed love and support. That night too, our bedroom window was open, and our daughter was changing her baby on our bed when she heard a whip-poor-will call again and again.

Days passed and our horrible pain continued. The day after Joel's funeral, his partner took out some old video footage. There on the footage was Joel whistling the whip-poor-will call to friends they were travelling with as a signal across a motel courtyard.

Joel and whip-poor-wills share certain similarities. Joel had very long eyelashes as do whip-poor-wills. A whip-poor-will is one of few birds that perch lengthwise on the branch instead of across, and Joel also tended to do things differently than others. Joel died because he flew his plane too close to the ground. The whip-poor-will is a very low flying bird.

In stories, the whip-poor-will has been called a goatsucker because it helps goats by eating insects on them, but the bird has been wrongly accused of sucking their milk. Some of the news reporting Joel's death distorted the image of who he really was. The media did not tell the story about the young man who was ever so loved by his family and friends. The man, like his Reykjavik ranching grandfather, protected the Canada geese; he was a gentle, caring rancher, a good neighbour, and father to a beautiful, long eye-lashed little girl who loved him beyond words.

Is all of this a brokenhearted mother? I think not. Joel had been referred to as "The Bird" for most of his life. Joel often repeated what he told me several times to be certain what he said was perfectly clear. Similarly, the whip-poor-will events were also repeated: the first visit to me, the second with witnesses, and the third when we watched the video showing Joel using the whip-poor-will-call.

People say that a whip-poor-will can sense a soul departing and can capture it as it flees.

Joel's message, via the whip-poor-will, that gives me tremendous peace is "all is well, mama—all is well."

And the quilt—

In 2007, we faced with trepidation our first Christmas without our son. My friend contacted my husband on 24 December to tell him that the quilt he had asked her to make for me years ago was ready. She had put in long hours to complete it for me by Christmas. My quilt holds thousands of stitches of love.

# About the Contributors

**Laura Apol** is the author of several award-winning poetry collections, and for years has conducted workshops to help facilitate healing through writing. Her daughter, Hanna, was at the centre of many of her poems. Since Hanna's death in April 2017, Laura is finding ways to use writing to express her own grief and to begin her own healing process.

**Antoine Babinsky** was born in Montreal in 1963. A member of the Royal Canadian Mounted Police for over thirty-one years, he retired in 2013 as an assistant commissioner. He is married and has been a grieving parent for more than five years.

**Andy Bond** and his wife Eileen are co-founders and current leaders of the Ottawa chapter of The Compassionate Friends of Canada. They are also TCF National Board members, and provide support to new and existing chapters across Canada. They have two surviving children and two grandchildren.

**Randie Clark** is a psychotherapist whose practice specializes in trauma, PTSD, and traumatic and complicated grief. She resides with her husband, and happily close to her daughter, son-in-law, and grandson. Randie co-authored the book, *When Your Child Dies, Tools for Mending Parent's Broken Hearts*, published in 2012.

**Suzanne Corbeil** is the proud mother of four adult children and two stepchildren. She lost her youngest child, Adam, when he was twenty-two. Suzanne and her husband Mike Robinson live in Ottawa, ON, where Suzanne runs a consulting company and finds solace in the garden she created in Adam's memory.

**Jane Davey-Keogh** has been a bereaved parent since 2004. She is a grief support group facilitator with Bereaved Families of Ontario-Ottawa region. Jane has connected with hundreds of bereaved parents by supporting them through offering her gift of grief experience, education, and wisdom gained.

**Elaine Dean** was born in the UK. Her family moved to Aurora, Ontario, before she started school. She moved to Ottawa after she graduated from university, where she lives with her husband Sean, her son Julian, and her mum Maureen.

**Ingrid Draayer**, a first-generation Canadian born to Dutch parents in Kingston Ontario, lives in rural Pakenham. Educated at the University of Toronto, she worked as a professional librarian at Carleton University Library for thirty-two years. Married to William Barrie, Ingrid is the mother of Jesse, Caitlin, and Brodie.

**Barb Duncan** grew up in Avoca, Québec. As a registered nurse, she worked at various nursing jobs, including the Rideau Carleton Raceway. Barb volunteers at a hospice in Renfrew and for Bereaved Families. Her children are Gordon, Andrew and Dana, who died. She loves to knit for her four grandchildren and four great-grandchildren.

**Stephanie Gilman** is a teacher and mother who supports others to reach their goals to the best of their ability. Stephanie enjoys music and theatre, the outdoors at all times of the year, spending time with friends old and new, and lots of laughter.

**Bonnie Hardy** married in 1972, and produced three Hardy boys: Trevor, Brendan, and Douglas. She has a diploma of acupressure, and was a colour and light meditation practitioner; she is currently a teacher of Jin Shin Do acupressure and has written articles for Jin Shin Do newsletters.

**Barb Hayduk** is an ordinary mother and former RCMP officer with a passion for community service. She learned the value of the written experience as part of her grief journey following the death of her beloved son, Chris. Barb hopes sharing her experience will help others.

**Jacquelyn Johnston** lives, works, plays, eats, sleeps, ponders and writes from an empty nest in a Vancouver suburb. She is writing a memoir about life with and without her children, whose memorials are in other suburbs she visits sometimes. She strives to discover the meaning of life and death.

**Susan Doyle Lawrence** became a bereaved mother in 1968 when her three-year-old son, Michael, disappeared from their yard; he was later found, drowned. The Compassionate Friends was founded in 1969, but it would be three decades before Susan would find TCF, after the death of her thirty-one-year-old daughter, Irene, in 1998, due to sudden undetermined natural causes. She serves on the National Board of TCF.

**Micheline Lepage** was born in Ottawa. She has worked in the high-tech sector as an event planner for most of her career. The death of her son changed her life in many ways, and she misses him deeply. She looks forward to seeing him again when God calls her home.

**Becky Livingston** hails from England. At twenty-four, she moved to Vancouver, B.C., and worked as an elementary school teacher for over twenty years. Her first book, *The Suitcase and the Jar: Travels with a Daughter's Ashes*, will be published in September 2018 by Caitlin Press. She currently lives and writes in Nelson, British Columbia.

**Judy Lynne** is retired and lives in Gibsons, British Columbia, where she facilitates a chapter of The Compassionate Friends. She is a member of the Sunshine Coast Threshold Singers who sing at the bedsides of those who are struggling with pain or nearing end of life.

**Judith Maguet** was born in 1951 on Vancouver Island. She and her husband raised their two sons and daughter on their mixed grain and cattle farm near Ste. Rose du Lac. They have two grandsons and three granddaughters. A love of children and a passion for gardening and reading have kept her heart happy.

**Tara McGuire** is a graduate of The Writer's Studio at Simon Fraser University and is now working on her MFA in Creative Writing at UBC. Her essays have been heard on CBC Radio and shortlisted by the Writer's Union of Canada. Tara lives with her husband and daughter under the tall trees of North Vancouver. www.taramcguire.com.

**Sylvia Pasher** trained as a computer programmer before the days of computer science degrees. She lived in Israel for twelve years where she married and where Daniel was born. They returned to Ottawa where her son Jonathan was born and where she worked as a research assistant and bookkeeper.

**Roy Patterson** has been happily married to Jane for thirty-eight years. He is the father of two sons, Ryan and Kevin. Kevin died in late 2015 at the age of thirty. Roy worked in the computer industry for forty years. Roy and Jane still struggle with the loss of Kevin and always will.

**Martha Royea** lives on the Sunshine Coast of British Columbia with her partner, her daughter and two dogs. She is grateful beyond words for the poets in her life. She practises and teaches Taoist Tai Chi, an activity that keeps her sane and grounded in a turbulent world.

**Donna McCart Sharkey** grew up in Montreal and now lives in Ottawa. She holds a PhD from the University of Ottawa, and her research includes studies conducted with war affected girls and young women. Her research has been published in numerous academic journals and she has contributed to various anthologies. Prior to retirement, she was a professor at The State University of New York. She is the mother of Alessandra and Renata.

**Cathy Sosnowsky** taught poetry as a college instructor for many years and started writing it after the freak accident of her teenage son in 1992. Later, she published *Holding On: Poems for Alex*. She continues to give workshops on writing as healing at many TCF gatherings.

**Lorna Thomas** is a storyteller. She has worked as a drama teacher, actor, and documentary filmmaker. Lorna is co-founder of the advocacy group Moms Stop The Harm. She enjoys singing and playing the ukulele, spending time with her daughter Cayley and husband Phil, and reminiscing about her beloved son Alex.

**Linda Turner** is a social work educator and practitioner in Atlantic Canada. She has worked in the palliative care field for the past five years. She and her partner Louis raised their family in the Acadian community of Rogersville, New Brunswick.

**Bonnie Waterstone** is a lesbian mother of two adult sons. David, the eldest, died 13 December 2014. She currently lives in, British Columbia, with her life partner. She is sustained by her Buddhist practice, singing in the Threshold Choir with Sunshine Coast Hospice, and kind friends.

**Lisa Whiteside** lives in Vancouver, British Columbia. She has three children: her son Sean, Lexi, who passed away on 23 January 2014, and Krista, who was Lexi's best friend. The two sisters had lived together in Vancouver and Edmonton. Lisa and her ex-husband Dave miss their daughter Lexi terribly.